READINGS ON EQUAL EDUCATION
(Formerly *Educating the Disadvantaged*)

READINGS ON EQUAL EDUCATION

Volume 19

PUBLIC POLICY AND COLLEGE ACCESS

INVESTIGATING THE FEDERAL AND STATE ROLES IN EQUALIZING POSTSECONDARY OPPORTUNITY

Volume Editor
Edward P. St. John

Series Editors
Charles Teddlie
&
Elizabeth A. Kemper

AMS PRESS, INC.
NEW YORK

READINGS ON EQUAL EDUCATION
VOLUME 19
Public Policy and College Access:
*Investigating the Federal and State Roles
in Equalizing Postsecondary Opportunity*

ISSN 0270-1448
Set ISBN 0-404-10100-3
Volume 19 ISBN 0-404-10119-4
Library of Congress Catalog Card Number 77-83137

All AMS Books are printed on acid-free paper that meets the guidelines
for performance and durability of the Committee on Production
Guidelines for Book Longevity of the Council on Library Resources.

AMS PRESS, INC.
BROOKLYN NAVY YARD, BLDG. 292, SUITE 417
63 FLUSHING AVENUE
BROOKLYN, NY 11205, USA

Manufactured in the United States of America

CONTENTS

VOLUME 19

CONTRIBUTORS' NOTES

WILLIAM E. BECKER is Professor of Economics at Indiana University, Bloomington, an adjunct professor at the University of South Australia, and executive editor of the Journal of Economic Education. Before joining the faculty of Indiana University in 1979, he was a tenured faculty member at the University of Minnesota, where he returned for the academic year of 1988 to serve as acting director of the Management Information Division. Bill has traveled worldwide on projects related to the economics of education and economic education and he has published extensively on related topics in numerous books and the major journals in economics and education. He is listed in *Who's Who in Economics* (4th edition, published by Edward Elgar Publishing Ltd).

CHOONG-GEUN CHUNG is a Statistician at the Indiana Education Policy Center at Indiana University in Bloomington. His research interests are statistical models for school reform, access and persistence in higher education, and issues in minority representation in special education.

BRIAN FITZGERALD has served as Staff Director of the Advisory Committee on Student Financial Assistance since March 1988. He also serves as adjunct associate professor of public policy at American University in Washington, D.C., where he teaches courses in the politics of public policy and education. For many years he has been involved in policy development and in research and redesign of student aid programs when he worked at Pelavin Associates, Inc., and Advanced Technology, Inc.

DONALD E. HELLER is Associate Professor and Senior Research Associate at the Center for the Study of Higher Education at Penn State University. Dr. Heller teaches and conducts research on issues relating to higher education economics, public policy, and finance, as well as academic and administrative uses of technology in higher education. The primary focus of his work is on issues of access and choice in postsecondary education, examining the factors and policies that help to determine whether or not individuals attend college, and what type of institution they attend.

JOHN B. LEE is currently the President of JBL Associates, Inc., an independent consulting firm that specializes in postsecondary education policy analysis. Previously, Dr. Lee worked for Abt Associates, the Education and Labor Committee of the U.S. House of Representatives, the Education Commission of the States, and Stanford Research International. He also spent time as an instructor, academic senate president, and president of the faculty union at Laney Community College in Oakland, California.

GLENDA D. MUSOBA is a Policy Analyst at the Indiana Education Policy Center and a doctorate candidate in higher education at Indiana University, Bloomington. Her research interests include access and equity in college admissions, student persistence, and other social justice issues.

EDWARD P. ST. JOHN is Professor of Educational Leadership and Policy Studies at Indiana University. His research focuses on the impact of school reforms and student financial aid on college access and other policy issues related to educational reform and finance. His most recent book is *Refinancing the College Dream: Access, Equal Opportunity and Justice for Taxpayers* (Johns Hopkins University Press).

ADA B. SIMMONS is the Associate Director of the Indiana Education Policy Center at Indiana University, Bloomington. Her research focuses on student persistence in higher education with an emphasis on financial factors, student involvement, and study patterns.

INTRODUCTION

PUBLIC POLICY AND COLLEGE ACCESS: INVESTIGATING THE FEDERAL AND STATE ROLES IN EQUALIZING POSTSECONDARY OPPORTUNITY

Edward P. St. John

This volume of *Readings on Equal Education* takes a critical look at how research informs policy development on college access. Since the early 1960s, differences in access for low-income and middle-income families have been an important issue. This policy issue was the impetus for the federal student aid programs that were created in the *Higher Education Act* of 1965. College enrollment rates for minority high school graduates and their White peers were nearly equal in the middle 1970s, largely as a consequence of federal need-based grants. However, a new inequality developed during the past two decades, substantially reducing enrollment opportunities for low-income students and creating a new disparity in enrollment (St. John, 2003).

In 1997, after a period of benign neglect of the role of finances in access, the National Center for Education Statistics (NCES) began publishing reports that built a new explanation for the new inequality in its access studies, an academic preparation rationale that focused on differences in preparation. Section I of this volume reviews the NCES studies illuminating the serious errors made in these studies. It also suggests remedies for the serious problems confronting policy research on access and persistence. The first four chapters show how these errors were made, consider the implications for federal higher education policy, demonstrate the critical need for a reanalysis of the NCES databases, and reanalyze the access challenge using NCES databases.

With the decline in federal student financial need-based grant aid since the late 1970s, states have been faced with the challenge of ensuring financial access and strengthening college preparation programs in high schools. Section II provides analyses of changes in the state role in promoting access to higher education. The chapters present evaluations of the impact of change in state policies on state student grant programs, academic preparation, and postsecondary encouragement.

In combination, these chapters suggest a new approach to policy research on college access and provide information on the impact of state and federal financial and school reform policies, issues considered in the concluding chapter. This introduction examines the emergence of the academic preparation rationale in education policy research before describing how this volume undertakes a critical examination of this research and its consequences for states.

The Federal Role

Historically, federal student aid programs were a catalyst for equalizing postsecondary opportunity in the U.S. However, this emphasis faded from the agenda of federal policy in favor of policies that promote school reform as a means of improving college access. The Advisory Committee on Student Financial Assistance, a Congressional panel, has provided leadership nationally in an effort to provide a more balanced approach to the study of college access. In a pivotal report, *Access Denied*, the Advisory Committee reanalyzed national reports on college access, reaching the following conclusion:

> Three decades ago, there was a unanimous agreement on the nation's access goal: low-income students who were academically prepared must have the same educational opportunity as their middle- and upper-income peers. Today, that opportunity—to pursue a bachelor's degree whether through full-time enrollment at a four-year institution directly upon graduation from high school or as a transfer from a two-year institution—is all but ruled out for increasing numbers of low-income students by record levels of unmet need. The rate at which academically qualified, low-income students attend four-year institutions provides one of the most sobering views of

America's educational and economic future. (Advisory
Committee on Student Financial Assistance 2001, p. vi)

In 2002, the Advisory Committee on Student Assistance
reanalyzed the first of the new NCES reports on college access
(NCES, 1997) and considered the implications of continuation of
these policies. Their report, *Empty Promises*, illuminated that large
numbers of low-income students would be left behind if there was
not a major infusion of funding in need-based grant programs.

In Chapter 1, Brian Fitzgerald summarizes key findings from
reports prepared by the Advisory Committee, *Empty Promises*,
and documented that the texts of NCES reports had been
deceptive. Using NCES's own statistical reports, the Advisory
Committee showed that a substantial percentage of low-income
and moderate-income college-qualified students were left behind
in the 1990s. Using these statistics, they estimated that about 4
million more students will be left behind in the first decade of the
twenty-first century. In addition to summarizing key findings from
this report, Fitzgerald describes why the Advisory Committee
decided to take a closer look at NCES reports on access and
persistence.

In Chapter 2, Donald Heller reexamines four NCES reports
on access and persistence. He examines their statistical methods
used in regression studies, considering the variables used in the
models and the variables that were left out. He identifies four
problems with the NCES reports: omitted bias, selection bias,
endogeneity bias, and collinearity. He illustrates how this
combination of statistical errors resulted in a misunderstanding of
the federal role in promoting college access.

In Chapter 3, William E. Becker considers the consequences
of these four statistical errors. He concludes that the NCES studies
omitted relevant financial variables and/or restricted their analysis
to only those students who were college-qualified. He provides an
econometric assessment of the consequences of omitting relevant
financial variables from a multivariate analysis of college-going
decisions, ignoring the sample selection problems and related
endogeneity issues associated with focusing only on those who are
college-qualified. NCES did not adequately consider the
implications of highly related variables that are believed to
influence college enrollment and persistence decisions. He
suggests how the NCES data should be re-analyzed to provide

consistent estimators of the relevant parameters in student-choice models of the college-going decisions.

In Chapter 4, John B. Lee presents a preliminary reanalysis of the National Educational Longitudinal Study (NELS), the database NCES analyzed in several of their reports on college access and persistence. Using two different methods of calculating college qualification—one limiting the population to students who had taken Algebra 2 and the other using a stricter set of criteria—Lee illustrates that a substantial percentage of low-income college-prepared students in the high school graduating class of 1992 were denied the opportunity to enroll in college, providing confirmatory evidence of the Advisory Committee's reinterpretation of NCES's statistics in *Empty Promises* (2002).

In combination these chapters confirm that there is a serious financial access problem in the U.S. Large numbers of college-qualified students have been and are being denied the opportunity to attend college because they lack the financial resources necessary to attend. In this political and financial context, states must fill the void of ensuring equal opportunity for college enrollment by students who take the steps to prepare for college.

The State Role

Given the failure of the federal government to maintain the national commitment to equal opportunity by providing adequate need-based aid, states are faced with critical policy choices about how to ensure access. Section II presents a series of evaluation studies that examine how well states promoted college access for low-income students in the new policy context of near benign neglect from the federal government.

In an effort to provide financial access to higher education, some states made substantial investments in need-based grant programs in the 1990s. In Chapter 5, Donald Heller summarizes research on the impact of state merit aid programs, research originally conducted by the Harvard Civil Rights Project. He reviews the development of new merit programs in the 1990s and summarizes evaluation studies of the impact of these programs. These analyses reveal that state funding for merit grants was associated with increased enrollment in public colleges, but these programs had a more substantial influence on enrollment by Whites than by African Americans.

In Chapter 6, an Indiana University (IU) research team presents the results of a study of the impact of state finance strategies on high school graduation rates and college enrollment rates in the states in the 1990s. The IU team assembled a state indicators database that was used in two analyses. The analyses of high school graduation rates examined the influence of annual current year tax rates, school funding, and college prices and grant aid (two years before graduation) on high school graduation rates, controlling to state demographic characteristics. The analysis of college enrollment rates for high school graduates examined the influence of state student grant programs, college prices, and tax rates, controlling for state demographic characteristics. These studies confirm need-based grant aid is essential to meeting the equal access goal in states.

Another set of initiatives in states in the 1990s focused on improving schools, as a means of promoting academic preparation. These policies included high-stakes exit exams, implementing math standards, and requiring advanced courses in high school math. In Chapter 7, the Indiana research team examined the influence of state reforms and school funding on three outcomes related to academic preparation—average SAT scores, high school graduation rates, and college enrollment rates—using a set of high school policy indictors and demographic indicators for the states in the 1990s. These analyses reveal that the linkages between education reforms and college access are far more complex than were envisioned by proponents of the excellence initiatives of the last two decades. While several of the new initiatives were associated with higher test scores, some were negatively associated with high school graduation rates. The excellence initiatives had little influence on the college enrollment rates for high school graduates.

It is also possible that states can improve college access using a comprehensive approach that combines school reform, postsecondary encouragement, and the guarantee of adequate grant aid. The state of Indiana's Twenty-first Century Scholars Program has provided this comprehensive approach for the past decade, a period in which Indiana rose from 47th among states in college access to 17th (St. John, Musoba, Simmons, & Chung, 2002). This program improved the odds that low-income students would prepare for and enroll in college. In Chapter 8, Glenda D. Musoba extends the research on the Twenty-first Century Scholars Program, examining the influence of the Scholars Program on

Whites and African Americans. The analysis reveals that Indiana's program has a more substantial influence on access for African Americans than Whites. However, the analysis also reveals the need to increase the involvement by minorities in urban communities.

Conclusions

In the final chapter, I review these analyses as a basis for suggesting future steps, and research and summarize how federal and state policy can facilitate improvement in access and equal opportunity in college enrollment. The reviews of NCES studies in Section I revealed serious shortcomings in evaluation research on college access. And while the chapters in Section II illuminate new approaches to assessing the effects of state level programs and policy, they do not fill the gap created by the flawed NCES studies. To facilitate further development in research, the concluding chapter addresses the critical challenge facing policy researchers by summarizing ways researchers can improve access research. In combination, the studies presented and summarized in this volume provide substantial information about the impact of state and federal policies related to college access. Therefore, the conclusion ends by summarizing how these studies can inform policy development.

References

Advisory Committee on Student Financial Assistance. (2001). *Access denied: Restoring equal educational opportunity.* Washington, DC: Author.

Advisory Committee on Student Financial Assistance. (2002). *Empty promises: The myth of college access in America.* Washington, DC: Author.

National Center for Education Statistics. (1997). *Access to higher postsecondary education for the 1992 high school graduates.* (NCES 98-105). By Lutz Berkner & Lisa Chavez. Project Officer: C. Dennis Carroll. Washington, DC: Author.

Sedlacek, W. E. (In press). *Measurement and evaluation in counseling and development.* San Francisco: Jossey-Bass.

St. John, E. P. (2003). *Refinancing the college dream: Access, equal opportunity, and justice for taxpayers.* Baltimore: Johns Hopkins University Press.

St. John, E. P., Musoba, G. D., Simmons, A. B., & Chung, C. G. (2002). *Meeting the access challenge: Indiana's Twenty-first Century Scholars Program.* Indianapolis, IN: Lumina Foundation for Education.

SECTION I

The Federal Role

CHAPTER 1

FEDERAL FINANCIAL AID
AND COLLEGE ACCESS

Brian Fitzgerald

Ensuring equal educational opportunity for all citizens represents the most important federal role in higher education. Since the passage of the Higher Education Act in 1965, need-based student financial aid has served as the primary federal policy instrument and policies have sought to ensure that students who otherwise could not afford to attend college have the financial resources to enroll and persist through degree completion. Grant aid is very important to low- and moderate-income students for whom a shortage of family financial resources constitutes the most important barrier to college—especially those among them who are academically prepared to attend a four-year college.

Today, the federal investment in student aid generates nearly $55 billion a year, including almost $12 billion in federal grants (College Board 2002a), which, augmented by need-based grant aid from states and institutions, lowers the price of college for needy students. The Federal Pell Grant program (Pell Grant), now the nation's largest need-based grant program, was designed in 1972 as a voucher which would ensure that students enjoyed both access to two-year and four-year public colleges and a modicum of choice between four-year public and private institutions. Access and choice would be achieved by the purchasing power of the maximum Pell Grant and the portability of the voucher, respectively (Wolanin, 2003). In most states and at the majority of

1

colleges, Pell Grants, with a maximum award of $4,050, represent the single largest source of grant funds with which to make college access for low- and moderate-income students a reality.

The recent transition to a knowledge-based economy has increased the demand for and the returns to college-educated workers, especially those with a bachelor's degree, have hit an all-time high, making these investments in student aid more important than ever. The returns to higher education for an individual today are greater than ever: workers with a bachelor's degree earn more than 75 percent more than workers with only a high school diploma (College Board, 2002b). Individual opportunity also builds an educated, highly skilled workforce, which has a powerful effect on national economic growth. These social and economic returns to higher education form the basis for our long-standing national commitment to and investment in equal access to higher education for all qualified students (Institute for Higher Education Policy, 2001; Kane, 1999).

The American ideal of individual educational opportunity has become a model for a host of nations, whether emerging from the long shadow of colonialism or from the grip of communism. Yet, at a time in which other nations have chosen to emulate our educational model, serious questions have emerged as to whether this model is really working for all Americans. Despite a growth in enrollments in higher education to an historic high of 15 million, gaps between the college-going rate of low-income and all other students are as wide today as thirty-five years ago when the nation first committed itself to equal educational opportunity for all (College Board, 2002b).

More systematic analyses have identified a persistent inequality of opportunity that faces low-income students. Data from a 1997 Department of Education study indicate that among low-income students with incomes of $25,000 or less: 65 percent earned a high school diploma: 34 percent graduated high school prepared for college: and only 17 percent ever attended a four-year college. This pattern is starkly different from that of high-income students with incomes of over $75,000: 95 percent earned a high school diploma: 82 percent graduated prepared for college: and 71 percent attended a four-year college (NCES, 1997). These and other studies have fueled a serious debate among researchers and policy makers concerning the causes of these inequalities: whether academic preparation, other factors, such as inequalities: whether academic preparation, other factors, such as information or finances, are to blame; and what policies can address these persistent inequalities. The centrality of access in the federal role creates an imperative for sound federal access research to guide federal policy.

The importance of federal access policy and the corresponding need for sound federal access research will increase dramatically over the course of this decade because powerful demographic forces already at work will increase the number of college-age Americans and change the face of American higher education. This demographic wave will add nearly 5 million 18-24 year-olds by 2015, 80 percent of whom will be minority and 50 percent Hispanic (Carnevale & Frye, 2002). This growth will cause the number of high school graduates to swell to unprecedented levels over the course of the current decade as the children of the baby boom generation and new immigrants flood high schools and colleges. Department of Education data indicate that this demographic trend will peak in 2008, when the largest number of students in the history of our nation will graduate from high school (U.S. Bureau of the Census, 2002). The ability of the largest generation in the history of our nation to gain access to college, and particularly a bachelor's degree, will determine the degree to which its members will have a realistic chance of joining the middle class.

Widespread school reform and early intervention efforts currently underway may substantially increase the proportion of high school graduates who are college-qualified. The *No Child Left Behind Act of 2001* committed the force of the state and federal governments to ensuring that all students receive a high quality education in elementary and secondary schools (U.S. Department of Education, 2003). This suggests that as school reform efforts take hold, increasing proportions of each high school graduating class may be prepared to attend college, further increasing the demand for higher education.

This record number of students will place even greater strains on our systems of higher education and higher education financing as demand exceeds the capacity of colleges and universities in many states and outpaces available student aid (California Postsecondary Education Commission, 2002). Higher education systems in key states most affected by this demographic growth, including California and Texas, cannot accommodate anticipated demand for seats. However, with deficits in the states running in the tens of billions of dollars, such aggressive plans appear unrealistic (Breneman, 2002a).

This demographic wave of students also will increase the demand for student aid dollars, since a higher percentage of these students will be from low-income, minority families. These students will be disproportionately dependent on grant aid. Students from low-income families will represent an ever-increasing proportion of high school students over future decades, and each successive graduating class will increase the demand for grant funds in order to make access to college and pursuit of a baccalaureate degree a reality (Advisory Committee on Student Financial Assistance, 2001). Over the past two years, the Federal Pell Grant program has faced a shortfall in excess of a billion dollars as eligibility for grants has exceeded appropriated funds (Morgan, 2002). At the state level, such growth in the demand for need-based grants will confront the commitment to merit aid in many states, as well as rising public-sector tuition—as much as 40 percent in several states--and reductions in need-based grant aid resulting from ballooning state deficits (Breneman, 2002a, 2002b; National Center for Public Policy and Higher Education, 2002; Russakoff & Argetsinger, 2003).

Consequently, the financial barriers confronting these students likely will rise significantly as demand for grants outstrips availability and as tuition rises as a result of the same deficits. If financial barriers rise, large numbers of additional low- and moderate-income students—beyond the millions identified above—will be denied access to a college education. Indeed, a recent update of the Texas higher education master plan indicates that Texas is far behind its existing goal of increasing Hispanic college attendance (Arnone, 2003; Murdock et al., 2002).

The Advisory Committee's Access Agenda

As a measure of Congress's commitment to college access, Congress created the Advisory Committee on Student Financial Assistance in 1986 and identified access as the Committee's primary purpose (20 U.S.C. 1098). Congress also charged the Advisory Committee with recommending "studies, surveys and analyses" that would serve to ensure that the needs of low-income students would be adequately measured and addressed. In anticipation of the reauthorization of the *Higher Education Act*, which likely will be completed in 2004, the Advisory Committee initiated a five-year agenda designed to conduct the most thorough assessment of college access and persistence for low- and moderate-income students in decades.

Three policy questions have dominated the Advisory Committee's access and persistence agenda:

- Does limited need-based grant aid—and the associated record-high net price of college (work and loan burden remaining after grants) facing low- and moderate-income high school graduates and their families—account for their significantly lower postsecondary enrollment and persistence rates?
- If so, how many low- and moderate-income high school graduates, especially among those who are college-qualified, are unable to enroll and persist in a college for which they are academically prepared?
- What are the national consequences of this shortfall in college enrollment and degree completion among low-income high school graduates?

These questions represent the essential questions for federal student aid policy and, consequently, federal access research. In order to address these questions, the Advisory Committee's analytic activities included:

1. Conducting an extensive review of literature and research;
2. Commissioning a set of scholarly papers on various dimensions of access;
3. Analyzing the most recent data available to assess the degree of access enjoyed by young Americans today; and
4. Evaluating federal access research.

This chapter reviews the results of these activities and assessments with a particular focus on important inconsistencies between the findings of Advisory Committee analyses and key findings of federally sponsored access research.

Access Research

The Advisory Committee's review of access literature and research uncovered a striking consensus among scholars and researchers regarding underparticipation of low-income students in higher education and the importance of family income and net price—college expenses remaining after student aid—for access.

Research documenting the under-participation of students from low-income families abounds. Despite a nearly forty-year commitment to educational opportunity the college enrollment gap between low-income and high-income students—the most widely used measure of college access—is as large today, 32 percentage points when compared to high-income students, as in the early 1970s (College Board, 2002a). Broad consensus exists among researchers that lack of access for low-income students is persistent and indeed may be worsening (Ellwood & Kane, 2000; Kane, 1994, 1999; McPherson & Schapiro, 1998, 1999; Mortenson, 2001a, 2001b; Orfield, 1992; Terenzini et al., 2001). Researchers also agree that the level of academic preparation, e.g., test scores, cannot explain the total difference in the college-going rate by family income (Cameron & Heckman, 1999, Ellwood & Kane, 2000; Kane 1998; Lee, 1999; McPherson & Schapiro, 1998, 1999). A substantial number of researchers have examined the importance of student aid and net price on decisions about postsecondary education (e.g., Jackson, 1978; Kane, 1999, 2002; Manski & Wise, 1983; McPherson & Schapiro, 1991, 1998; St. John, 1994a, 1994b; Terenzini et al., 2001). In particular, research has demonstrated that low-income students are highly sensitive to net price and changes in net price (Cameron & Heckman, 1999; Dynarski, 1999; Heller, 1997, 2001; Jackson, 1978; Leslie & Brinkman, 1987; Manski & Wise, 1983; McPherson, 1988; McPherson & Schapiro, 1991, 1998; St. John, 1990).

The enrollment effects of federal financial and other aid programs can be traced through various steps in the education or "college access" pipeline. As early as eighth grade, enrollment effects can be seen in the expectations that students hold for enrolling in college. Likewise, enrollment effects of federal financial aid programs are evident in high school seniors' plans for college, admissions test taking, college application submissions, and, ultimately, enrollment in college (Hossler et al., 1999).

Indeed, all of the steps in the access pipeline leading up to an enrollment decision (e.g., expectations, plans, test taking, and applying) are influenced by financial aid. King (1996) found that low-income students who expected to receive financial aid were more likely to aspire to college than were other low-income students. Additionally, knowledge about financial aid can increase the number of higher education options that a student considers.

Flint (1992) showed that knowledge of financial aid allowed families to consider a wider range of institutions and influenced their financial planning. In sum, the perception of the availability of financial aid encourages expectations of matriculation for students, particularly those from low-income families (Hossler et al., 1999; Jackson, 1978; King, 1996; Olson & Rosenfeld, 1984; St. John, 1994a, 1994b; St. John et al., 1996; Terenzini et al., 2001). These researchers concluded that the simple presence of financial aid, and the success that follows, is enough to encourage students to prepare for college and to take the steps necessary for enrollment in an institution.

However, a student's reliance on financial aid varies in direct proportion to family income, with low-income families relying on financial aid the most (Miller 1997). NCES (1997) found that, of all income levels of students, the lowest socioeconomic students reported being much more concerned about financing their education when choosing a school. Tierney (1980) and Leslie, Johnson, and Carlson (1977) also indicated that the probability of a low-income student attending college could be influenced by the perception that financial aid was available. For the students in middle school and high school, financial aid is extremely important to enable low-income students to actualize the goal of achieving access to higher education. Tierney (1980) echoed the findings of Leslie, Johnson, and Carlson (1977) by showing that higher-SES students have greater access to information sources about financial aid than do the lowest-SES students. Since financial aid makes college seem possible, knowledge of it causes students to engage in the behavior necessary for college matriculation, such as taking college preparatory courses, completing college admissions tests, and enrolling in early intervention programs.

In addition to the indirect effects of aid on the earlier stages of the pipeline, one of the most visible effects of student aid programs is that they increase overall, measurable enrollment decisions among low-income families. These families are the most price sensitive of all families (Cameron & Heckman, 1999; Dynarski, 1999; Heller, 1997, 2001; Jackson, 1978; Leslie & Brinkman, 1987; Manski & Wise, 1983; McPherson, 1988, 1999; Rouse, 1994; St. John, 1990). As Jackson (1978) found, increases in financial aid lead to an increase of students enrolling in college. Manski and Wise (1983) estimate that the Pell program raised low-income student enrollment by 60 percent more than it would have been without the program, although this estimate is disputed (Hansen, 1983). Kane (2001, 2003) documents the increase in enrollments, but cites the complexity of the student aid system as a factor limiting the effectiveness of student aid. In examining state grant aid, Kane (2003) estimated that the Cal Grant entitlement increased enrollment among applicants by 3 to 4 percent. Likewise, financial aid can impact the choices that low-income students have.

The lowest-SES students at four-year public institutions were three times more likely (74 versus 28 percent) than the highest-SES students to claim that financial aid is very important in their choice of institution (Terenzini et al., 2001). Kane (2003) also found that higher levels of Cal Grants increase the likelihood of recipients to attend private colleges.

Financial aid also counters the negative impact that tuition increases have on students. Heller (1997) concluded that every net tuition increase of $100 leads to a decline in enrollment from .5 to 1 percentage points. In addition, McPherson and Shapiro (1998) estimated that a $150 net cost increase (in 1993-94 dollars) would result in a 1.6 percentage point decline in enrollment among low-income students, suggesting that a $1000 (in 1982-83 dollars) increase in tuition would depress total enrollment by about 3 percentage points. However, the negative impact of one dollar of tuition increase is neutralized by the positive effect of one dollar of grant aid (Manski & Wise, 1983). Ellwood and Kane (2000) estimated that a $1000 increase in subsidy (thereby lowering tuition) would increase enrollment by 5 percent.

These findings suggest that financial aid is most effective for low-income students because they are highly responsive to net prices and would have lower probabilities of enrolling in college in the absence of financial aid. From perceptions of financial aid in eighth grade to enrollment decisions following high school graduation, financial aid has a positive impact on the enrollment steps of the education pipeline, particularly for low-income students.

Persistence Effects

In addition to the positive effects that financial aid has for student entry into college, receipt of aid enables greater persistence throughout a student's undergraduate career, the next steps along the education pipeline. Financial aid effects persistence decisions positively through maintenance of equilibrium between the net price of attending college and the perceived economic returns to the attainment of a degree. Persistence effects include measured reductions in dropout rates, transfer rates from community colleges to four-year institutions, and institutional investment in need-based student aid. Positive effects on persistence are particularly important in evaluating the effectiveness of aid programs because the benefits of higher education cannot be fully realized if students are unable to graduate and obtain degrees.

Jensen (1981) and Murdock (1987) found that financial aid promotes student persistence. As with matriculation findings, financial aid is more effective for low-income students' persistence than for the persistence of other students from other income categories. In a 1995 study, the General Accounting Office found a 14 percent reduction in the dropout probability of low-income students with the addition of a $1,000 grant (United States General Accounting Office, 1995). Moreover, this study found that if grants were targeted to first year low-income students, an additional $1,000 in grant aid reduced their probability of dropping out in the first year by 23 percent.

Other evidence of the effectiveness of the financial aid programs comes from the greater probability that aid recipients are more likely to transfer from a community college to a four-year campus than are non-recipients (Murdock, 1987). Since attendance at a four-year institution is necessary for the attainment of a bachelor's degree, the impact of financial aid on transfer rates is extremely important.

When considering the effectiveness of financial aid programs, researchers often debate which programs best promote persistence. Specifically, researchers have found that grants are more effective than loans at keeping students, particularly those from low-income families, in college (Jensen, 1981; Stampen and Cabrera, 1987; United States General Accounting Office, 1995). In general, low-income students are very responsive to grants whereas loans and work-study programs do not have as large an impact (Terenzini et al., 2001).

Whether the researchers look at enrollment or persistence effects of financial aid, the general conclusion is clear—financial aid programs enable low-income students to complete the educational pipeline and graduate from college. Although federal financial aid programs may not be adequately funded, and therefore unable to fully achieve their goal, the programs have provided access to millions of students and have the potential to further reduce the current inequities in access that face our nation. This body of research formed the foundation for the Advisory Committee's own research and analysis, described below.

Advisory Committee Access Findings

The Advisory Committee reexamined the most current data available to assess the state of access for low- and moderate-income students today. These analyses resulted in the release of two reports, one of which, *Empty Promises: The Myth of College Access in America (2002),* is reviewed in this section.[1]

Figure 1. Average Annual Unmet Need Facing High School Graduates by Family Income and Type of College (Full-time, Dependent Students).

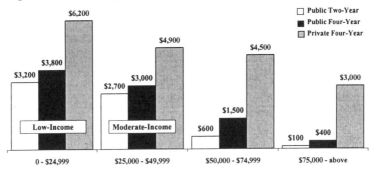

Source: U.S. Department of Education, NCES (1999)

Taken together, these two reports demonstrate that two decades of underfunding grant aid and substituting loans, tax credits and merit-based aid has erected very substantial financial barriers to college for low- and moderate-income students, the most price sensitive of all students. As a result, unmet need—the portion of college expenses not covered by what the family can reasonably pay for college, the so-called expected family contribution (EFC), and student aid, including work-study and loans—has reached unprecedented levels. On average, annual unmet need for low-income families in the late 1990s reached $3,200 at community colleges, $3,800 at four-year public colleges, and $6,200 at four-year private colleges (Figure 1). By contrast, high-income families face only $400 in unmet need at these four-year public colleges.

However, this gap between college expenses and financial aid belies the true magnitude of the financing challenges facing these families. Most low-income families are able to contribute only a small portion of college expenses and, consequently, the real financial barrier is total college expenses minus all grant aid. Yet, grants comprise only about one-third of total student aid, and the work-study and loan portions of a student's aid package can be substantial, at least $1,000 in work-study and $2,625 in loans for freshmen, and often much higher (Figure 2). This gap between grant aid and college cost represents the true net price of college for these students and the barrier that must be overcome before access to college can become a reality.

Figure 2. Work and Loan Burden Facing Low-income Families with High Unmet Need at a Typical Four-year Public College.

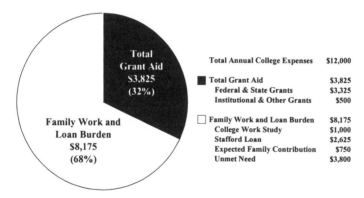

In the face of these financial barriers, work is an essential component of many low-income students' financing strategies, but one that often lowers the probability of degree completion considerably. Sixty-five percent of all low-income college students work while enrolled, on average 24 hours a week, although nearly a third work more than 35 hours a week; and 80 percent of students enrolled at two-year public colleges work an average of 27 hours a week (NCES, 1997). For low-income students, such decisions are less a choice and more an inevitable response to high levels of unmet need. Excessive work reduces persistence and degree completion from 79 percent for low-income students who work relatively few hours to 47 percent for students who work more than 35 hours a week (Advisory Committee on Student Financial Assistance, 2001).

Inadequate grant aid has increased annual borrowing among low-income students throughout the 1990s, which rose 65 percent to $3,000 in annual borrowing and increased cumulative debt 50 percent to $15,000. Low-income minority students, in particular, borrow at much higher rates than high-income students and often much more than all other students; 71 percent of low-income students graduate with debt as compared with 44 percent of high-income students. African American students borrow $2,000 more than other students and over half of both African American and Hispanic students graduate with debt levels that are considered unmanageable by student loan industry standards (US PIRG, 2002).

Moderate-income students, with income between $25,000 and $50,000, confront similar financial barriers: $2,700 in unmet need at community colleges, $3,000 at four-year public colleges, and $4,900 at four-year private colleges. They also face very high work and loan burden at public colleges: $5,641 a year at public four-year colleges (see Figure 1).

Impact on Student Enrollment Behavior

The barriers of unmet financial need and work/loan burden represent key factors in determining whether high school graduates have access to a four-year public institution and a bachelor's degree. Focusing on high school graduates provides the opportunity to isolate the effects of unmet need from those of academic preparation and other factors on college-going behavior.

The most effective means of assessing the impact of financial barriers on student behavior is to focus on those students who graduate from high school academically prepared to attend a four-year college. All of the students in this analysis were qualified to and planned to attend a four-year college immediately after graduation, and were well informed about college costs and financial aid. These factors suggest that they are highly likely to attend four-year colleges.

Figure 3. The Full Access Pipeline (College-qualified High School Graduates).

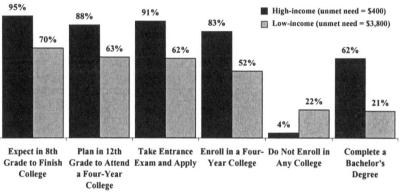

Source: Calculated from data in U.S. Department of Education, NCES (1997) and (2002)

High financial barriers affect college-qualified, low-income students at many steps leading up to college enrollment. Because many find it financially impossible to plan to attend a four-year college or to attend college immediately following graduation, they neither test nor apply to college six times as often as their high-income peers and apply to a four-year college at only two-thirds the rate of their high-income peers. These barriers, however, have their clearest effect on college enrollment decisions: 48 percent of these college-qualified students do not attend a four-year college within two years of graduation and 22 percent attend no college at all (Figure 3).

These enrollment differences do not narrow, even among the most highly qualified students. Among those high school graduates who are highly and very highly qualified, high-income students attend a four-year college at a rate that is 43 percent higher than their low-income counterparts—67 percent versus 47 percent.

The highest achieving poor students attend college at the same rate (78 percent) as the lowest achieving wealthy students (77 percent). And 23 percent of the highest achieving poor students do not attend college compared with only 3 percent of the highest achieving wealthy students who do not attend college (Figure 4).

Figure 4. Impact of Socioeconomic Status and Family Income on the Most Highly Qualified High School Graduates.

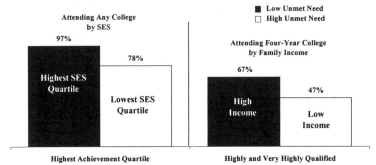

Source: Lee (1999) and U.S. Department of Education, NCES (1997)

As in the case of low-income high school graduates, the financial barriers confronting college-qualified, moderate-income high school graduates have a substantial and comparable impact on their expectations, plans, and enrollment behavior: 43 percent do not enroll in a four-year college within two years of graduation and 16 percent do not attend any college at all (Figure 5).

Thus, the impact of unmet need on the behavior of college-qualified, low- and moderate-income high school graduates is substantial and does not decline as the level of academic preparation increases. These data suggest that adequate academic preparation or other factors such as information cannot inoculate high school graduates against the debilitating effects of significant financial barriers.

Figure 5. Comparison of the Impact of High Unmet Need On the Behavior of Low- and Moderate-income (College Qualified) High School Graduates.

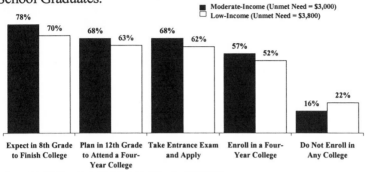

Source: Calculated from data in U.S. Department of Education, NCES (1997)

The substantial proportion of college-qualified, low- and moderate-income high school graduates who are unable to enroll in a four-year college—or any college at all—suggests that large numbers of students were denied access to college in 2001-2002: 406,000 college-qualified high school graduates from low- and moderate-income families were prevented from enrolling in a four-year college, and 168,000 of them did not enroll in any college at all (Figure 6).

Figure 6. Total Impact of High Unmet Needs on Low- and Moderate-income (College Qualified) High School Graduates in 2001-2002.

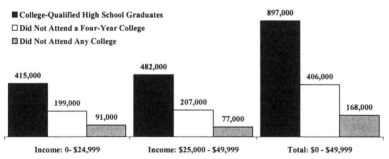

Source: Calculated from data in U.S. Department of Education, NCES (1997) and (2001)

This large group of college-qualified low- and moderate-income high school graduates who are denied access today also portends very substantial losses over the course of this decade: 4.4 million students will not attend a four-year college; and 2 million students will not attend any college at all (Figure 7). This staggering toll suggests that one of the core values we hold as a nation, equal educational opportunity, starkly contrasts with the reality of opportunity in America today.

Figure 7. Cumulative Impact of High Unmet Need on Low- and Moderate-income (College Qualified, in Millions) High School Graduates From 2001-2010.

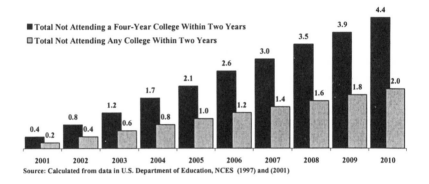

Source: Calculated from data in U.S. Department of Education, NCES (1997) and (2001)

Federal Access Research

These findings from the Advisory Committee's two reports, *Access Denied* and *Empty Promises*, supported by a broad consensus among researchers, contrasts sharply with the findings and conclusions from recent federal access research conducted by the Department of Education's National Center for Education Statistics (NCES). Over the last decade, NCES has conducted several analyses of longitudinal data designed to measure the impact and adequacy of financial aid on the college-going behavior of low-income high school graduates. Congress and the Secretary of Education require such studies to inform federal higher education, and in particular, access policy. Indeed, in its seminal study, "Access for 1992 High School Graduates," NCES (1997) acknowledges the importance of access by noting:

1. "The distinct differences in enrollment patterns by family income are consistent with a common perception that high costs deter low-income students from attending postsecondary education at all, and if they do attend, deter them from enrolling in four-year institutions where the tuition is higher." (p. 9)
2. "There is little doubt that the cost of attending postsecondary education posed difficulties for low-income 1992 high school graduates, and while financial aid reduced the differences in the amounts required to attend different types of institutions, on average, several thousand dollars remained to be paid." (p. 14)

Recent NCES *tabular* analyses (e.g., 1997, 2000) of the college-going behavior of low-income high school graduates have included the following explanatory factors: college costs, student aid, family income, race/ethnicity, parents' education, and student academic qualifications. The treatment of college costs and student aid have involved two price measures and their relationship to college-going behavior: unmet need—college cost net of financial aid and expected family contribution—and net price—college cost net of financial aid. The use of both measures has been responsive to the need of policymakers to assess the impact and adequacy of financial aid. NCES's tabular analyses using these measures have been consistent with theory and empirical research indicating that unmet need and net price are strongly related to differences in college-going behavior of high school graduates by family income. Both the analyses and the findings have been consistent also with theory and empirical research indicating that the college-going behavior of high school graduates is also related to family income, race and ethnicity, parents' education, and academic qualifications.

Unlike its tabular analyses, NCES multivariate analyses of the college-going behavior of high school graduates have excluded unmet need, net price, and student aid; that is, these important factors were not used as explanatory variables in those analyses and, accordingly, have never been found to be related to college-going behavior of high school graduates. The rationale that has been offered for the exclusion of these factors as explanatory variables has been that NCES did not examine the effects of college costs or financial aid on high school graduates who did not apply for and attend college. This rationale, in effect, has precluded multivariate analysis of the effects of college cost and student aid on the college-going behavior of low-income high school graduates, despite the fact that underlying tabular analyses suggest that unmet need and net price are strongly related to that behavior.

Thus, while NCES's multivariate analyses have found that the college-going behavior of high school graduates is related to family income, race/ethnicity, parents' education, and academic qualifications, those analyses have not directly explored the relationship between college-going behavior and *any* measure of price net of student aid or student aid itself. More importantly, these analyses have failed to identify the large population of low-income high school graduates who are college-qualified but do not attend college, and fail to explore why they do not attend, a crucial part of the task of assessing the impact of financial aid on low-income students, and assessing the adequacy of financial aid as well.

An Overly Restrictive Definition of Equal Access

The problems with NCES analyses of access and persistence began with a highly restrictive definition of access in the 1997 NCES report "Access to Postsecondary Education for the 1992 High School Graduates" (NCES 1997). That report focused on those 1992 high school graduates who were considered "college qualified" because they possessed adequate academic preparation, grades, and test scores to gain admission to most four-year colleges. In addition, the analyses focused almost exclusively on those college-qualified students who had taken a college entrance exam and had applied to a four-year college. Not surprisingly, the study defined equal access as "no substantial differences by family income in the four-year college enrollment rates of such students" (NCES 1997, p. 1-2). This overly restrictive definition of equal access departed from the prevailing definition of access both inside and outside NCES. Most notably, it screened out over 80 percent of the low-income students in the sample, effectively eliminated family income, college costs, and financial aid as causal factors, and guaranteed a finding that access was in fact equal. Ironically, under this definition, it could be asserted that access was equal *before* passage of the Higher Education Act in 1965.

Further, while the study was designed in large part to determine whether high net prices (college costs minus financial aid) accounted for the lower college enrollment rates of low-income high school graduates, the regression analyses found that "other factors" were to blame, including not only academic preparation but also a series of "steps": student educational expectations and plans, and testing for and applying to a four-year college. Most notable was the finding that low-income high school graduates—even those whose parents had low levels of education—were able to attend four-year colleges at the same rates as students from middle-income families "if they do what four-year colleges expect them to do" (p. iii)[2].

There were four serious methodological problems underlying these findings:

First, available amounts of financial aid and net college costs were never used as independent variables in the regression analyses. Thus, those analyses could not have assessed whether those factors did in fact account for the lower postsecondary enrollment rates of low-income high school graduates.

Second, if financial aid was excluded, it follows logically that the analyses could not have assessed whether family income—inversely related to financial aid—accounted for those lower rates.

Third, educational expectations and plans and academic preparation were not, in fact, independent "other factors;" both were strongly related to family income in the study data, as well as to available amounts of financial aid and net college costs, excluded from the equations.

Fourth, taking the steps required to be admitted to a four-year college was not an appropriate independent variable because it was itself a function of the dependent variable in the equations: the decision to attend a four-year college or not.

These methodological errors seriously undermine the validity of the finding that access was equal and financial aid adequate to permit low-income students to enroll in college.

A Follow-up Study in 2000

NCES published *Mapping the Road to College: First-generation Students' Math Track, Planning Strategies, and Context of Support* (NCES 2000). Like NCES 1997, NCES 2000 excluded any measure of college costs, financial aid, or net price as an independent variable. Unlike NCES 1997, it did not focus exclusively on college-qualified high school graduates, or include taking the steps required to be admitted to a four-year college as an independent variable.

However, like NCES 1997, along with family income, it used educational expectations of parents and students as an independent variable, along with a long list of other factors, many of which were very likely strongly related to family income, including: college qualifications, level of ACT/SAT preparation, extracurricular activities, etc. The addition of these variables as regressors could significantly reduce the estimated effect on enrollment of family income—already minimized by the exclusion of financial aid. The authors recognized this impact and warned the reader that adding regressors related to family income served to minimize the measured effect of differences in family income, although they nevertheless emphasized that their regression analyses in fact corroborated the finding of NCES 1997 that access was equal for low-income students.

NCES's 2001 Synthesis

NCES published a summary essay in *The Condition of Education,* entitled "Students Whose Parents Did Not Go to College." To synthesize ten years of its own access and persistence research—the multivariate analyses which had excluded finances as explanatory factors and had found family income not to matter—NCES 2001 focused exclusively on the role of parents' education. The essay failed to acknowledge that the underlying studies had found that the effects of parents' education on enrollment were quite modest and both positive and negative, depending on the level of education and the type of college involved. The essay relied on bivariate estimates to find that the likelihood of enrolling and persisting in college was strongly related to parents' education even when other factors were taken into account. However, as in the underlying studies, there appeared to be no consideration of college costs, financial aid, or net price; and there was neither an examination of the role of family income on enrollment, the bivariate estimates for which were as high as those for parents' education, nor of any interaction effects between family income and parents' education.

Finally, the essay failed to note the contradictory findings in the tabular analysis in the 1997 study: that virtually no difference existed between the enrollment rates of college-qualified, low- and middle-income high school graduates.

Advisory Committee External Review

In light of these serious methodological weaknesses in and conflicting findings among recent NCES studies, the Advisory Committee initiated an external review of these studies to resolve inconsistencies with Advisory Committee analyses and several decades of research. In particular, the external review focused on the fact that while excluding unmet need, net price, and student aid from its multivariate analyses of the college-going behavior of high school graduates, the NCES studies nevertheless included findings that access was equal, financial aid was adequate, and, by inference, family income did not play as significant a role in college access as previous research had indicated. In particular:

1. NCES found no significant differences between the four-year-college enrollment rate of low- and middle-income high school graduates who are college-qualified, and "do what colleges tell them to do," that is, in spite of their parents' low-income and education (NCES, 1997, p. iii).
2. In a synthesis of its own multivariate analyses, NCES found that parents' education is equally as likely as family income to have caused a gap of over thirty percent in postsecondary enrollment between college-qualified low- and high-income high school graduates (NCES, 2002).

These two conclusions taken together, in light of the exclusion of net price, unmet need, and financial aid from the multivariate analyses in these studies, appear inconsistent with over thirty years of economic research as well as the tabular analyses in both studies.

These inconsistencies suggested three research questions as the focus on the external review of this research:

1. Are NCES's tabular analyses in studies over the last decade consistent with prevailing theoretical and empirical views of the importance of family income, net price, unmet need, and financial aid on college-going behavior of low-income high school graduates?

2. Are NCES's multivariate analyses and findings consistent with those views and NCES's own tabular analyses?
3. Are NCES's multivariate analyses and findings methodologically sound?

The subsequent two chapters explore these questions in depth and discuss the implications for the validity and policy relevance of the conclusions of these studies.

Acknowledgement

The author gratefully acknowledges the contribution of William Goggin, who conducted the reanalysis of the NCES 1997 data and Kirstin McCarthy who assisted with the bibliography. The views expressed in this chapter are those of the author and no official support of the Advisory Committee on Student Financial assistance or other government entity is intended or inferred.

Notes

1. The data included in *Empty Promises* result from a reanalysis of NCES 1997. All data presented in this section are from this report, unless otherwise noted.
2. In a June 13, 2002 letter, Thomas Kane, Professor of Public Policy at UCLA, responded to the claim above in the following way:

> The conclusion that income may be an obstacle in clearing the earlier hurdles but that income is not an obstacle to enrolling once the other barriers have been cleared is simply not supportable with such evidence. The problem is known within the social sciences as resulting from "selection bias." ... The suggestion in the publication that if only low-income students could be made to satisfy the other requirements, they could expect the same college-going rates as the low-income students who currently clear those hurdles [result of selection bias]. ... This confusion about the implications of selection bias pervades the [NCES] publication "Access to Postsecondary Education for the 1992 High School Graduates."

Kane further explains that this is more than an academic quibble. If the NCES and ACE conclusions are correct, there are strong policy implications: "There would be little reason to raise the Pell Grant if the important hurdles are earlier in the process."

References

Advisory Committee on Student Financial Assistance. (2001). *Access denied: Restoring the nation's commitment to equal educational opportunity.* Washington, DC: Author.

Advisory Committee on Student Financial Assistance. (2001). *Estimating the impact of unmet need on college qualified students.* Washington, DC: Author.

Advisory Committee on Student Financial Assistance. (2002). *Empty promises: The myth of college access in America.* Washington, DC: Author.

Arnone, M. (2003). Texas falls behind to enroll more minority students. *The Chronicle of Higher Education, 49*(19), A 23.

Breneman, D. W. (2002a). For colleges, this is not just another recession. *The Chronicle of Higher Education, 48*(40), B 7.

Breneman, D. W. (2002b, Spring). Declining access: A potential—if slow moving—train wreck. *National Crosstalk, 11*(2), 11-12.

California Postsecondary Education Commission. (2002). *The California Postsecondary Education Commission's public agenda: Priorities for action.* Commission Report 02-5. Sacramento, CA: Author.

Cameron, S. V., & Heckman, J. J. (1997). Can tuition policy combat rising wage inequality? In M. Kosters (Ed.), *Financing college tuition: Government policies and educational priorities* (pp.76-124). Washington, DC: American Enterprises Institute.

Carnevale, A. P., & Fry, R.A. (2000). *Crossing the great divide: Can we achieve equity when Generation Y goes to college?* ETS Leadership 2000 Series. Princeton, NJ: Educational Testing Service.

College Board. (2002a). *Trends in student aid, 2002.* Washington, DC: Author.

College Board. (2002b). *Trends in college pricing, 2002.* Washington, DC: Author.

Dynarski, S. (1999). *Does aid matter? Measuring the effect of student aid on college attendance and completion.* Working Paper No. 7422. Cambridge, MA: National Bureau of Economic Research.

Ellwood, D. T., & Kane, T. J. (2000). Who is getting a college education? Family background and the growing gaps in enrollment. In S. Danziger & J. Waldfogel (Eds.), *Securing the future: Investing in children from birth to college* (pp. 283-324). New York: Russell Sage Foundation.

Flint, T. A. (1992). Parental and planning influences on the formation of student college choice sets. *Research in higher education, 33*(6), 689-708.

Heller, D.E. (1997). Student price response in higher education: An update to Leslie and Brinkman. *Journal of Higher Education, 68*(6), 624-659.

Heller, D.E. (2001). *The effects of tuition prices and financial aid on enrollment in higher education: California and the nation.* Cordova, CA: EdFund.

Hossler, D., Schmit, J., & Vesper, N. (1999). *Going to college: How social, economic, and educational factors influence the decisions students make.* Baltimore, MD: The Johns Hopkins University Press.

Institute for Higher Education Policy. (1998). *Reaping the benefits: Defining the public and private value of going to college.* The New Millennium Project on Higher Education Costs, Pricing, and Productivity. Washington DC: Author.

Jackson, G. A. (1978). Financial aid and student enrollment. *Journal of Higher Education, 49*(6), 549-574.

Kane, T. J. (1994). College attendance by blacks since 1970: The role of college cost, family background, and the returns to education. *Journal of Political Economy, 102*(5), 878-911.

Kane, T. J (1999). *The price of admission: Rethinking how Americans pay for college.* Washington, DC: Brookings Institution Press.

Kane, T. J. (2001). Assessing the American financial aid system: What we know, what we need to know. In M. Devlin (Ed.), *Forum futures 2001: Exploring the future of higher education* (pp. 25-34). Cambridge, MA: Forum for the Future of Higher Education.

Kane, T. J. (2003). *A quasi-experimental estimate of the impact of financial aid on college-going.*

Working Paper No. 9703. Cambridge, MA: National Bureau of Economic Research.

Kennedy, P. (1992). *A guide to econometrics*. Cambridge, MA: The MIT Press.

Lee, J. B. (1999). How do students and families pay for college? In J. E. King (Ed.), *Financing a college education: How it works, how it's changing* (pp. 9-27). Phoenix, AZ: The American Council on Education and The Oryx Press.

Leslie, L. L., & Brinkman, P. T. (1987). Student price response in higher education: The student demand studies. *Journal of Higher Education, 58* (2), 181-204.

Leslie, L. L., Johnson, G. P., & Carlson, J. (1977). The impact of need-based student aid upon the college attendance decision. *Journal of Education Finance, 2*(3), 269-85.

Manski, C., & Wise, D. (1983). *College choice in America*. Cambridge, MA: Harvard University Press.

McPherson, M. S. (1988). On assessing the impact of federal student aid. *Economics of Education Review, 7*(1), 77-84.

McPherson, M. S., & Schapiro, M. O. (1991). Does student aid affect college enrollment?: New evidence on a persistent controversy. *American Economic Review, 81*(1), 309-318.

McPherson, M. S., & Schapiro, M. O. (1991). *Keeping college affordable*. Washington DC: Brookings Institution.

McPherson, M. S., & Schapiro, M. O. (1998). *The student aid game: Meeting need and rewarding talent in American higher education*. Princeton, NJ: Princeton University Press.

McPherson, M. S., & Schapiro, M. O. (1999, May). *Reinforcing stratification in American higher education: Some disturbing trends*. Macalester Forum on Higher Education Conference, Diversity and Stratification in American Higher Education, St. Paul, MN.

Miller, E. I. (1997). Parents' views on the value of a college education and how they will pay for it. *Journal of Student Financial Aid, 27*(1), 20.

Morgan, R. (2002). $1.4-Billion Deficit Prompts Debate Over Pell Grants. *The Chronicle of Higher Education, 49*(6), A28.

Mortenson, T. G. (2001a, October). College participation by family income, gender and race-ethnicity for dependent 18 to 24 year olds 1996 to 2000. *Postsecondary Education OPPORTUNITY, 114*, 1-8.

Mortenson, T. G. (2001b December). Family income and higher education opportunity 1970 to 2000. *Postsecondary Education OPPORTUNITY, 112*, 1-9.

Murdock, S. E., White, S., Hoque, N., Pecotte, B., You, X., & Balkan, J. (2002). *The Texas challenge in the twenty-first century: Implications of population change for the future of Texas.* College Station, TX: The Center for Demographic and Socioeconomic Research and Education.

National Center for Public Policy and Higher Education. (2002). *Losing ground: A national status report on the affordability of American higher education.* San Jose, CA: Author.

Olson, L., & Rosenfeld, R. A. (1984). Parents and the process of gaining access to student financial aid. *Journal of Higher Education, 55*(4), 455-480.

Orfield, G. (Fall 1992). *Money, equity, and college access.* Harvard Educational Review, Vol.62 No.3. Cambridge, MA: President and Fellows of Harvard College.

Pascarella, E., & Terenzini, P. (1991). *How college affects students: Findings and insights from twenty years of research.* San Francisco, CA: Jossey-Bass.

Perna, L.W. (2002). Pre-college outreach programs: Characteristics of programs serving historically underrepresented groups of students. *Journal of College Student Development, 43*(1), 64-83.

Rouse, C. E. (1994). What to do after high school: The two-year versus four-year college enrollment decision. In R. G. Ehrenberg (Ed.), *Contemporary policy issues in education* (pp. 85-96). Ithaca, NY: ILR Press.

Russakoff, D., & Argetsinger, A. (2003, July 22). States plan big tuition increases. *The Washington Post*, p. 1.

St. John, E.P. (1990). Price response in persistence decisions: An analysis of the high school and beyond sophomore cohort. *Research in Higher Education, 31*(4), 387-403.

St. John, E.P. (1991). What really influences minority attendance? Sequential analyses of the High School and Beyond sophomore cohort. *Research in Higher Education, 32*(2), 141-158.

St. John, E.P. (1994a). Accessing tuition and student aid strategies: Using price-response measures to simulate pricing alternatives. *Research in Higher Education 35*(3), 301-335.

St. John, E.P. (1994b). *Prices, productivity, and investment: Assessing financial strategies in higher education.* ASHE-ERIC Higher Education Reports, No. 3. Washington, DC: The George

Washington University, ERIC Clearinghouse on Higher Education.

St. John, E. P., Paulsen, M. B., & Starkey, J. B. (1996). The nexus between college choice and persistence. *Research in Higher Education, 30*(6), 563-581.

Stampen, J. O., & Cabrera, A. F. (1988). The targeting and packaging of student aid and its effect on attrition. *Economics of Education Review, 7*(1), 29-46.

Terenzini, P. T., Cabrera, A. F., & Bernal, E. M. (2001). *Swimming against the tide: The poor in American higher education.* The College Board Research Report no. 2001-1. New York: The College Board.

The Institute for Higher Education Policy. (2001). *Rhetoric and reality: Effects and consequences of the HOPE scholarship.* The New Millennium Project on Higher Education Costs, Pricing, and Productivity. Washington, DC: Author.

Tierney, M. S. (1980). The impact of financial aid on student demand for public/private higher education. *Journal of Higher Education, 51*(5), 527-545.

Tuma, J., & Geis, S. (1995). Student financing of undergraduate education, 1992-93 (NCES 95-202). Washington, DC: U.S. Department of Education, National Center for Education Statistics.

U.S. Bureau of the Census. (2001). School enrollment in the United States—Social and economic characteristics of students (P20-533). Washington, DC.

U.S. Department of Education. National Center for Education Statistics (1997). *Access to postsecondary education for the 1992 high school graduates* (NCES 98-105). Washington, DC: Author.

U.S. Department of Education. National Center for Education Statistics. (2000). *Mapping the road to college: First-generation students' math track, planning strategies and context of support.* (NCES 2000153). Washington, DC: Author.

U.S. Department of Education. National Center for Education Statistics. (2001). *The condition of education 2001* (NCES 2001-072). Washington, DC: Author.

U.S. Department of Education. (2002). *Strategic plan 2002-2007.* Washington, DC: Government Printing Office.

U.S. General Accounting Office. (March 1995). *Higher education: Restructuring student aid could reduce low-income student dropout rate.* (GAO/HEHS-95-48). Washington, DC: Author.

US PIRG. (2002). *The burden of borrowing. A report on the rising debt rates of student loan debt.* The State PIRG's Higher Education Project. Washington, DC: Author.

Wolanain, T.R. (2003). *Reauthorizing the Higher Education Act: Issues and options.* The Institute for Higher Education Policy. Washington DC: The Institute for Higher Education Policy.

CHAPTER 2

NCES RESEARCH ON COLLEGE PARTICIPATION: A CRITICAL ANALYSIS

Donald E. Heller

Introduction[1]

In recent years the National Center for Education Statistics (NCES) has issued a series of reports focusing on access to postsecondary education. Using a number of analytical tools and textual descriptions, these reports describe the relationship between a number of factors, such as student and institutional characteristics, and other factors, such as whether students enroll in college, what type of college they attend, and whether they persist to degree attainment.

Some of the NCES findings provide contradictory evidence of the relationship between financial characteristics, including family income, tuition prices, and the availability of financial aid, and the college participation rate of low-income students. In particular, the findings from tabular analyses often contradict that from multivariate analyses.

With Congress and the Administration debating the reauthorization of the Higher Education Act of 1965 (HEA) this year, it is important to understand this conflict. Title IV of the HEA authorizes the federal student aid programs, including the Pell and Supplementary Educational Opportunity Grants, the Perkins, Ford Direct, and Family Education Loan programs, and the College Work Study program. These programs together made available over $54 billion in aid to students in the 2001-2002 academic year, or 61 percent of all financial aid (College Board, 2002).[2]

Thus, the federal government makes a substantial investment and has a vested interest in ensuring that these funds are used to promote the goals articulated in HEA over 35 years ago:

> It is the purpose of this part to provide, through institutions of higher education, educational opportunity grants to assist in making available the benefits of higher education to qualified high school graduates of exceptional financial need, who for lack of financial means of their own or of their families would be unable to obtain such benefits without such aid (*Higher Education Act of 1965*, [Pub. L. No. 89-329(1965)]).

The goal of this study is to examine in detail four primary NCES reports that focus on college participation, and analyze the nature of the conflict, if any, between the results of the tabular and multivariate analyses in these reports, as well as between those results and the findings of other researchers on college access.[3] The specific questions addressed in this chapter include:

- whether the NCES tabular analyses in these studies are consistent with prevailing theoretical and empirical views of the importance of family income, net price, unmet need, and financial aid on college-going behavior of low-income high school graduates;
- whether the NCES multivariate analyses and findings are consistent with those views and the NCES tabular analyses; and
- whether the NCES multivariate analyses and findings are methodologically sound.

The results of this study will help explain this conflict, as well as provide recommendations for further research that can help explain the effectiveness of financial aid in promoting college participation for students with different socioeconomic characteristics.

Following this introduction, the second section provides a brief overview of the existing empirical research, other than the four NCES reports, on the relationship between a number of variables and college participation. The third section summarizes the findings of the NCES tabular analyses and compares those findings to other research on college participation. The fourth section summarizes the findings of the NCES multivariate analyses, and in similar fashion, compares those findings to other research on college participation.

The fifth section of the chapter provides a more detailed critique of the methodological approach used by NCES in its multivariate analyses, with a focus on understanding why the results conflict with the findings in the tabular analyses. The sixth and final section makes some recommendations for future research that could provide more evidence of the role of financial aid in promoting college participation.

Previous Research on College Participation

A broad body of research on college participation in the United States exists, much of which focuses on the relationship between student and family characteristics and the decision to enroll in and persist through college. Many of these studies also examine the role of financial aid in helping students to overcome the cost barriers that inhibit them from participating in postsecondary education. This section briefly summarizes this research and its key findings.

Tabular Analyses

Concerns over the relationship between family financial resources and college participation long preceded the HEA. In a study in the early part of the twentieth century, Morey (1928) described the potential discouragement effect on college enrollment of fees charged at public institutions, and the need for financial aid to overcome that effect. After World War II, President Harry Truman's Commission on Higher Education expressed concerns similar to those addressed nearly twenty years later in the HEA:

> For the great majority of our boys and girls, the kind and amount of education they may hope to attain depends, not on their own abilities, but on the family or community into which they happened to be born or, worse still, on the color of their skin or religion of their parents. (President's Commission on Higher Education, 1947)

Analyses of the college participation rates of students from different socioeconomic groups have documented the long-standing gaps that exist among these groups. These gaps have persisted at all measurement points of the postsecondary education attainment process: in high school graduation rates,[4] in college entry rates, in college persistence rates, and in degree attainment rates. For example, while students from all income groups have seen gains in these rates in the three decades since passage of the HEA, the gaps between high-income and low-income students have stubbornly persisted.

Thomas G. Mortenson, in his newsletter *Postsecondary Education OPPORTUNITY*, has long tracked these gaps using Census Bureau data. His most recent analysis (Table 1) describes the gaps at some of these points (Mortenson, 2001b). Low-income students are less likely to continue through each point in the educational pipeline, and the gap between low- and high-income students increases through later stages of the pipeline. The Census Bureau's own reports confirm these gaps; for example, the high school dropout rate of students from families making less than $20,000 in 1999 was more than three times the rate of students from families making over $40,000 (United States Bureau of the Census, 2001).

Table 1. Educational Attainment Rates of Highest and Lowest Income Quartiles Groups, 2000.

Measure	Highest Income Quartile	Lowest Income Quartile	Difference
High school graduation	92%	65%	27 points
College entry from high school	82%	54%	28 points
Bachelor's degree attainment	52%	7%	45 points

Dependent students age 18 to 24
Source: Mortenson, 2001b

The gaps in postsecondary participation and attainment found among individuals from different income groups are found also when students with other socioeconomic characteristics are compared. Race and ethnicity is another important correlate of educational attainment. Mortenson (2001a) also examines this relationship and reports large differences in college participation among the groups. Among dependent 18 to 24-year-olds, the college participation rates are as follows: whites, 64 percent; Asian/Pacific Islanders, 78 percent; blacks, 46 percent; and Hispanics, 40 percent.[5] As with the gaps in participation among different income groups, these racial/ethnic gaps have similarly persisted for decades (Clotfelter, 1991; Heller, 1999; Koretz, 1990). That Asian American and white families have much higher incomes, on average, than black and Hispanic families is, no doubt, an important factor in explaining the racial gap in college participation; thus, the strong correlation between race and income in the United States.

Mortenson (1999b) also documented the relationship between parental education levels and college participation. As the education level of a student's mother, father, or guardian increases, the probability that the student would enroll in college also increases.

Multivariate Analyses of the Relationship Between Socioeconomic Status and College Participation

There are strong relationships among the various measures that are often included under the label "socioeconomic status." As described above, race and income are strongly correlated in the United States. Similarly related is the relationship between educational attainment and income. As has been documented in numerous reports, people with higher levels of education earn more money.[6] And as has been described above, students from families with more money are more likely to participate in college.

In order to separate the effects of these collinear relationships, numerous researchers have conducted multivariate analyses of the relationship between socioeconomic status and college participation. Using a number of factors, including such measures as race, family income, pre-college academic achievement, parental education, tuition prices, and financial aid offers, researchers attempt to gauge the effect each has on the probability that a given individual will enroll in or persist through college.

The results of these studies are fairly consistent; controlling for other factors, researchers generally have found the following factors related to college participation:

1. Higher levels of family income are related to a higher probability of college participation (Jackson, 1989; Manski & Wise, 1983; St. John, 1991);
2. Higher levels of parental education are related to a higher probability of college participation (Ellwood & Kane, 2000; Jackson, 1989); and
3. Higher levels of academic achievement are related to a higher probability of college participation (Behrman, Kletzer, McPherson, & Schapiro, 1992; Rouse, 1994; St. John, 1990).

It is important to note that the findings regarding the relationship between socioeconomic status and college access hold even when the student's academic preparation is taken into account. In an analysis of data from the National Education Longitudinal Study (NELS) of 1988, Kane (1999) divided students into quartiles based on their score on math tests administered as part of that study. Even for students in the top test score quartile, i.e., those who were the most academically qualified, he found a large gap in the probability that the student would enroll in college when comparing those from the lowest family income group and those in the highest family income group. This gap between rich and poor still existed when he used class rank as the indicator of academic achievement, rather than test scores.[7]

In addition to these findings, researchers have examined the relationship between tuition prices, financial aid, and postsecondary participation. Three reviews of this literature in the last three decades (Heller, 1997; Jackson & Weathersby, 1975; Leslie & Brinkman, 1988), which cumulatively examined over 150 studies, have reached the following conclusions:

1. The college participation rate of low-income students is most responsive to increases in tuition prices; high-income students show little responsiveness to higher tuition prices in their college *entry* decisions, though their college *choice* decisions can be influenced by changing prices; and
2. The awarding of financial aid, and, in particular, grants, is related to higher probability of college participation for low-income students (i.e., grant aid can offset at least some of the impact of rising tuition prices); as income increases, the enrollment responsiveness of

students to financial aid offers decreases. Financial aid can affect the college *choice* decisions of higher income students, however.

Review of NCES Tabular Analyses

This review examines the following NCES reports on college access:

1. Berkner, L., & Chavez, L. (1997). *Access to postsecondary education for the 1992 high school graduates* (NCES 98-105).
2. Choy, S. P. (2001). *Students whose parents did not go to college: Postsecondary access, persistence, and attainment* (NCES 2001-126).
3. Horn, L., & Nuñez, A.-M. (2000). *Mapping the road to college: First-generation students' math track, planning strategies, and context of support* (NCES 2000-153).
4. Wei, C. C., & Horn, L. (2002). *Persistence and attainment of beginning students with Pell Grants* (NCES 2002-169).

For the sake of brevity, each report in the remainder of this review will be referred to as Report 1, Report 2, Report 3, and Report 4, respectively.[8]

The sources of the data for the analyses in these NCES reports are the following longitudinal surveys conducted for NCES:

- NELS of 1988, which included students in the eighth grade in 1988, with follow-up surveys in 1990, 1992, 1994, and 2000 (Reports 1, 2, and 3);
- Beginning Postsecondary Students (BPS) Longitudinal Study, which included students beginning postsecondary education in either the 1989-90 or 1995-96 academic years. The first cohort was surveyed again in 1992 and 1994, and the second cohort was resurveyed in 1998 (Reports 1 and 4); and
- Baccalaureate and Beyond Longitudinal Study, which included students completing a bachelor's degree in the 1992-93 academic year, with follow-up surveys in 1994 and 1997 (Report 2).

In addition, supplementary information from the National Postsecondary Student Aid Study (NPSAS) was used to provide comparison data in some of the reports.

The Relationship Between Family Income and College Participation

The tabular analyses of the relationship between family income and college participation conducted by NCES confirm the findings of the research reported in section two of this report: students from high-income families are more likely to enter college than are students from low-income families.[9] In Report 1, students graduating from high school in 1992 are divided into three income groups: those from families making less than $25,000 (28 percent of all students); from families making $25,000 to $74,999 (57 percent); and from families making $75,000 or more (15 percent). While 37 percent of low-income students had not enrolled in any form of postsecondary education within two years of high school graduation, only 21 percent of middle-income students and 7 percent of high-income students had not entered higher education within that same time period. These differences are also evident in the type of institution attended for those students who did enroll in postsecondary education. Eighty-two percent of high-income students who enrolled in college attended a four-year institution, while only 51 percent of low-income students were enrolled in this sector.

Detailed comparisons of these figures with research conducted by others on this relationship is difficult, because of differences in time periods studied, as well as differences in defining family income groups. However, the pattern reported by NCES in its tabular analyses is consistent with that of other researchers: low-income students are less likely to attend college than their peers from wealthier families, and when they do, they are less likely to be enrolled in a four-year institution.

The Relationship Between Parental Education and College Participation

As with income, parental education is a strong correlate of college participation. NCES Reports 1, 2, and 3 show the following percentages of students graduating high school in 1992 who did not enroll in college within two years: students whose parents were high school graduates or less, 41 percent; some college, 25 percent; college graduates, 8 percent.[10] Again, these results are consistent with the bivariate analyses conducted by others and described in section two of this report.

The Relationship Between Financial Aid and College Participation
The four NCES reports reviewed in this study provide limited tabular data regarding financial aid and college participation. For example, Report 4 focuses exclusively on Pell Grant recipients, so by nature of its sample it excludes many middle- and most all high-income students. In addition, it only analyzes those students who enrolled in college. Report 1 includes financial aid data only for low-income students (below $25,000), but it does not distinguish between students who did or did not receive a financial aid offer from a university and whether the students enrolled in college or not. In the many reports issued based on data from the NPSAS surveys (Berkner, 1998; Berkner, Berker, Rooney, & Peter, 2002; Tuma & Geis, 1995), NCES does provide much detailed data on the distribution of financial aid to students with different socioeconomic characteristics. But because these studies only examine students already enrolled in college, they are unable to provide information on the relationship between financial aid and college participation.

Review of NCES Multivariate Analyses

As described in section two of this report, multivariate analysis allows the researcher to examine the simultaneous effects of a number of characteristics on a chosen outcome, or in the vernacular of research, to examine the effect of one factor while controlling for others. Multivariate analysis is particularly powerful when these factors, or predictors of the outcome, are interrelated, a condition quite common among student background characteristics such as race, family income, and levels of parental education.
Reports 1, 3, and 4 all provide multivariate analyses of an outcome related to college participation.[11] Reports 1 and 3 focus on enrollment in college within two years of high school graduation as the outcome, while Report 4 focuses on continuous enrollment in college through 1998 for those students who began in the 1995-96 academic year. Two predictors, family income and parental education level, appear in the analyses in all three reports.[12] Other predictors appear in only one or two of the three

reports, and include such variables as race, gender, an index of "college qualification," educational expectations, and whether the student took a college entrance examination.

It is clear from the organization of the NCES reports that the multivariate analysis is not the centerpiece of the analysis; in each of the three reports, the multivariate analysis is relatively brief and is the final section before a concluding chapter. Nevertheless, the findings of the multivariate analyses are often discussed in the textual description of the reports, including the executive summary or highlights sections.

Multivariate Findings Regarding Income, Parental Education, and College Participation

Since income and parental education level are factors included in all three reports, these findings will be discussed first. As reported in section three of this report, the NCES tabular analyses report large differences in college entry (Reports 1 and 3) and college persistence (Report 4) among students from different income groups as well as among students whose parents had differing levels of educational attainment themselves.

The approach of the NCES multivariate analyses is to measure the predicted outcome (college enrollment or persistence) as one factor among a number of predictors, and then report "adjusted percentages" of the outcome for each characteristic after controlling for these other factors. The adjusted percentages can then be compared to the raw, or unadjusted, outcome percentages, for each factor. Figure 2 summarizes the adjusted percentage for income and parental education in these three reports.

Table 2. Adjusted College Participation Percentage by Income and Parental Education Level.

	Report 1		Report 3		Report 4
	Attended community college	Attended four-year institution	Attended other than four-year institution†	Attended four-year institution	Persisted through 1998
Income					
Low	21.9*	42.2*	49.8	44.3*	54.8*
Middle	**28.6**	**44.7**	58.3	44.8*	**59.3**
High	22.9*	52.3*	**57.8**	**56.9**	‡
Parental Education					
HS grad or less	23.0	41.0*	**49.3**	**42.3**	56.6
Some college	28.5*	42.8*	56.9*	43.6	54.7*
College graduate	**24.9**	**50.6**	61.9*	51.1*	**59.4**
Advanced degree					65.2*

Notes
Referent groups are shown in bold; * p ≤ 05 (compared to referent group).
Other variables included in the multivariate models varied in each report, but included measures such as race, gender, age, college-qualification index, taking steps toward four-year college (entrance examinations and applying), type of high school (public or private), and parents' educational aspirations for their children.
The income groups are as follows:
Reports 1 and 3, low: <$25,000; middle: $25,000 - $74,999; high: >$75,000
Report 4, dependent students: low, <$25,000; middle: $25,000 - $69,999
Report 4, independent students: low, <$6,000; middle: $6,000 - $24,999
† For those who did not enroll in a four-year institution.
‡ This report focused on Pell Grant recipients; it includes only low- and middle-income students.

These results indicate that, controlling for other factors, family income and parental education are still predictors of college participation. For example, Report 1 indicates that high-income students were more likely to attend a four-year institution within two years of high school graduation, and low-income students less likely than their middle-income peers. Report 3 indicates that both low- and middle-income students were less likely to attend a four-year institution than their high-income peers. Report 4 shows that low-income students were less likely to persist for three years continuously than their middle-income counterparts.[13]

The effects of parental education are similar. Reports 1 and 3 show that students whose parents were college graduates were more likely to enroll in a four-year institution than were those whose parents had less education. The results regarding the effect of parental education on persistence were more mixed. Students whose parents had an advanced degree were more likely to persist than those whose parents had only a bachelor's degree, and those whose parents had attended college without attaining a bachelor's degree were less likely to persist. Interestingly, those students whose parents had never attended college had persistence rates that were not statistically different from those whose parents held a bachelor's degree. A possible explanation for this result (though evidently not tested in Report 4) could be that students with parents who had no college experience had overcome such high barriers just to get to college that the drive and motivation to be successful once there was as great as that of students whose parents had higher levels of educational attainment.

Report 2 focuses exclusively on the role of parental education in explaining postsecondary participation as well as post-baccalaureate outcomes. While the report draws largely on analyses conducted in the other three reports, the way that the analyses are recounted may be misunderstood by some readers. For example, on page seven a highlighted statement indicates that, "the likelihood of enrolling in postsecondary education is strongly related to parents' education *even when other factors are taken into account*" (emphasis added). Yet the data provided to support this claim are tabular analyses of the relationship between parental education and college entry from Reports 1 and 3 that *do not* control for other factors. In fact, the multivariate analysis in Report 3 indicates that when the outcome is entry into a four-year college or university, there is no statistical difference between students whose parents had never attended college and students whose parents had some college experience, but had not attained a bachelor's degree, a finding that is acknowledged later in Report 2.

In another section of Report 2, the author summarized the findings regarding parental education and college persistence, stating that, "students whose parents did not attend college remain at a disadvantage with respect to staying enrolled and attaining a degree...again controlling for other related factors" (p. 4). Yet Report 4 demonstrates that this is not true, as Table 17 of that report shows that there is no statistical difference in three-year persistence rates between students whose parents had no college experience and those whose parents had a bachelor's degree after controlling for other factors, including family income.[14] This also may lead readers to draw an incorrect conclusion regarding the relationship between parental education and college participation when other factors are taken into account.

Multivariate Findings Regarding College Costs, Financial Aid, and College Participation

The NCES reports have very little to say regarding the role of financial aid and the cost of college in encouraging or discouraging college participation.[15] In some cases, this appears to be because of a limitation of the surveys used and resulting data elements available to the report authors. For example, Report 1, which uses data from NELS, notes in the multivariate analysis chapter that, "financial aid was not included as a variable because the amounts are known only for those who enrolled [in college]" (p. 67). In other words, data about financial aid awards was only collected for those NELS students who enrolled in college, and not for those who may have been offered financial aid but chose not to enroll in college. Similarly, information about the cost of college was available only for students who enrolled in college, but not for those students who may have been accepted at one or more colleges, but chose not to enroll.

In the one report where detailed financial aid and college cost information was available, the authors chose not to include the breadth of data available to them when conducting the multivariate analyses. In the multivariate analysis of persistence in Report 4, which included low- and middle-income students, the only measure of college costs or financial aid that was included was the receipt of a Pell Grant during the first year of college. No other financial aid variables, such as loans, state grants, institutional grants, or other aid, were included as a control variable, nor was any measure of the cost of college, such as tuition, cost of attendance, or net price, included. The authors do not state why these variables were omitted from the analysis.

The omission of financial aid and college cost variables from the multivariate analyses is troubling given other information in these reports. Report 1 has a chapter on differences regarding concerns about paying for college among students from different socioeconomic groups. For example, Table 27 in this report indicates that while only 20 percent of high-income students and 16 percent of their parents were "very concerned about college costs and availability of financial aid," 69 percent of low-income students and 79 percent of their parents were similarly concerned. So while the impact of finances on students' college enrollment decisions is not clear because the authors did not report on this linkage, it is clear that there are differences in the expressed concern about finances among these different groups of students. While the NELS study has very little information about financial aid, the BPS study does provide detailed financial aid information for each student. This information could have been used to expand the analyses in Report 4 to better account for the role of different forms of financial aid on persistence.

Analysis of NCES Methodological Approach

The NCES College Qualification Index

In analyzing the effect of socioeconomic status on college participation, the NCES and the authors of its reports have attempted to address an important consideration: all students are not equally qualified, nor necessarily equally motivated, to attend postsecondary education. In order to understand the impact of a number of these factors on college participation it is important to try to separate those students who could not or would not attend college because of other reasons, and focus on the remaining students.

The approach that NCES has taken to perform this separation is to label students as "college qualified" based on high school grades, class rank, courses taken, and aptitude test scores, including tests administered for the NELS survey as well as SAT and ACT tests. In addition, Report 1 also includes two additional steps by examining "those students who had the initiative to take a college entrance exam and submit an application for admission to a four-year institution" (p. 1).

The relationship between family income and each of the steps toward becoming college-qualified can be gleaned from some of the NCES reports. Report 1 creates a five-level scale based on a composite of the academic measures described earlier. The distribution of all 1992 high school graduates in the three income groups is shown in Figure 3.[16] Close to half of all low-income students (income below $25,000) were considered only marginally or not qualified for a four-year institution and thus excluded from being labeled "college-qualified," in contrast to fewer than 15 percent of the high-income students ($75,000 or more).

Figure 3. Proportion of 1992 High School Graduates by Income and College Qualification Index.

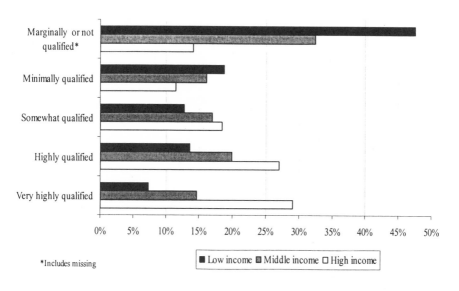

*Includes missing

■ Low income ▨ Middle income ☐ High income

Source: Report 1, Table 14.

Similar differences were reported by NCES when Report 1 examines the steps taken toward attending college, taking a college entrance examination, and applying to a four-year institution by those students who were college-qualified. For example, while 62 percent of low-income students accomplished both of these steps, 91 percent of high-income students did both. Nineteen percent of low-income students took neither step, while only three percent of high-income students failed to do either (Report 1, Table 22).

Even among those students who were in the marginally or not college-qualified category (all of whom the authors label "not college-qualified"), the high-income students were more successful at finding their way into some form of postsecondary education. Seventy percent of high-income students who were *not* college-qualified still attended some form of postsecondary education within two years of high school graduation, and almost half of those attended a four-year institution. Less than half of low-income students who were not college-qualified attended college, and less than a quarter of those who did enrolled in a four-year institution (Report 1, Table 33).

The Problem With Focusing on "College-Qualified" Students

Controlling for this separation of college-qualified students from those who were not college-qualified, a key conclusion reached by the authors of the NCES reports can be found in the highlights section of Report 1:

High school graduates whose parents have low levels of income and education are able to attend four-year colleges at the same rates as students from middle-income families, if they do what four-year colleges expect them to do. That is, if low-income students have an academic record and aptitude test scores which demonstrate even the minimal qualifications for admission to a four-year institution, if they take a college entrance examination, and if they submit an application for admission, the majority of low-income students enroll in postsecondary education, and over 83 percent attend a four-year college or university (p. iii).

Report 3 echoes this finding:

> After adjustment, however, low- and middle-income students enrolled [in four-year institutions] at similar rates. This last finding may reflect the leveraging effect of financial aid in providing access to college for low-income students (p. 54).

These passages say that those low-income students who managed to get themselves "college-qualified" by taking the steps and achieving the academic standards outlined in the reports had college participation rates similar to those of their middle-income peers.[17] This implies that college finances, i.e., the cost of college and availability of financial aid, are not a barrier to the participation of low-income students, at least as compared to middle-income students.

This is an important consideration given the concern about college finances among students from different income groups that was reported earlier.[18] However, the analysis in the NCES reports does not attempt to incorporate this concern and measure its impact on college participation. The multivariate analyses of the impact of financial aid on college participation that have been conducted by other researchers and summarized in section two have generally found that financial aid *does* influence the enrollment and persistence of low-income students, even controlling for academic skills and abilities.

The first problem posed by the analytic approach chosen by NCES is that its methodology ignores the role that college finances may have on the decisions made or efforts performed by students to make themselves "college-qualified." In other words, if students and their parents are discouraged early in their high school careers from attending college because they believe it is financially out of reach, then they may not take the steps necessary to put themselves into this college-qualified pool. This series of sequential steps, many dependent upon successful completion of the earlier ones, sets up a screening mechanism that may exclude all but the most determined students who somehow are able to overcome the price signals they receive from the higher education market.

For example, if high tuition prices and lack of information about financial aid as early as the middle school years discourage a low-income student from considering college as an option, then she is not likely to take the college preparatory course sequence defined by NCES. If the student does not take this course sequence, then it is unlikely she will, one, score at the level necessary on the aptitude tests administered by NCES to satisfy the test score criteria for college qualification, and, two, be encouraged to take a college entrance examination. And if she does not take a college entrance examination, or score at a sufficient level on one of these tests, then it is unlikely she will be encouraged to apply to a four-year institution.

The implications of the NCES approach can be seen in Figure 1. At any of these points, students who did not believe they could ever go to college because of financial barriers, despite their aptitude to be successful in college, could make decisions or perform academically in ways that would serve to lower their final college qualification ranking. These decisions or performance levels could have cumulative effects toward lowering the index value. The decision not to apply to a four-year college or to take a college entrance examination tags a student as not qualified for college in some of the NCES analyses. It is important to remember again that there were large differences among income groups in these college qualification indices. While 86 percent of high-income students were at least minimally "college qualified," only 53 percent of low-income students achieved this standard (Report 1, Table 15).

A second problem with the approach taken by NCES is that it ignores the unmeasured differences between those students who managed to get themselves "college-qualified" (including those who also took the SAT or ACT test and applied to a four-year institution) and students who could not achieve this standard. These unmeasured variables may include factors such as internal or external motivation or "push" to attend college[19], assistance on college planning from peers, teachers, counselors, or others[20], and competitive spirit. It is reasonable to expect that those students who were able to make themselves college-qualified by the NCES standard, and, in particular, low-income students, differed not just in their academic talents, but also in possessing a higher level of something a generation or two ago called "gumption." The unmeasured differences between these students and the resulting impact on the multivariate analyses are described by researchers as "selectivity" or "self-selection" bias.

Figure 1. Sequential Steps in NCES Definition of Being "College Qualified."

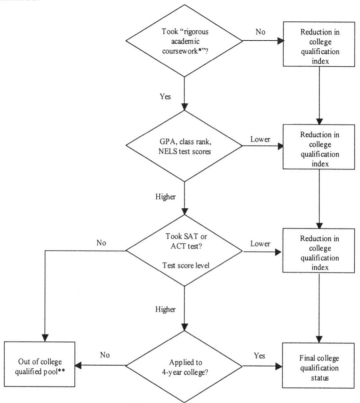

*   At least four years of English, three years each of science, math, and social studies, years of foreign language (Report 1, p. 24)
**   Some of the NCES analyses exclude students who did not complete these two steps.

By including the successful completion of these hurdles as a criterion for later measurement as part of the college participation pool, the NCES methodology introduces a serious limitation in its analysis. The decisions of students to overcome these hurdles, or their ability to do so, cannot simply be included as a minimal threshold before their postsecondary experiences can be related to their background characteristics, such as family income and parental education. This methodology treats the steps toward college-qualification (defined by academic achievement, taking college tests, and applying to a four-year college) as exogenous variables that are independent of the other factors that help determine whether one goes to college or not. But as described earlier, they are not exogenous, but, rather, endogenous to the decision to enroll in college.

By not attempting to measure the impact that concern over college finances may have on low-income students, or by not mentioning more prominently the potential of this impact, the authors of these reports may inadvertently be misleading readers about the role of family income on college participation. From the quote excerpted from Report 1 above, it would be reasonable for a reader to conclude that all the efforts of federal, state, or private programs should focus on getting these low-income students college qualified; i.e., if we could just solve that problem, then the gaps in college participation outlined in section two of this report could be eliminated.[21] Yet it is not known from these reports whether lessening the concerns regarding college finances of low-income families—by lowering college costs, by increasing the availability of financial aid, by providing better information about aid, and the like—would have a similar or perhaps even greater impact on eliminating the college participation gap.

The third problem with the NCES college-qualification index is its assumption that the index represents the steps necessary for a student to be prepared for enrollment in a four-year college or university. While this may be in part true, it represents a very traditional path toward college entry, a path that has undergone great change in recent years and is likely to change even more in the future.

A report by the National Center for Fair & Open Testing (Rooney & Schaeffer, 1998) listed almost three hundred schools that have eliminated the requirement of students submitting SAT or ACT scores, made them optional, or deemphasized their use in the admissions process for at least some entering students.

Included are major university systems such as the public university system in Texas and the California State University system. In addition, many colleges have alternative admissions programs for some students who may score well below the institutional norms on the standard criteria of high school grades, class rank, and college entrance examination tests. While many of these changes have been made subsequent to the cohort of students analyzed in the NCES reports (the high school graduating class of 1992), it is still important to note that the ways in which many students become "college-qualified" today are quite different from those assumed by the NCES methodology.

The Problem With Focusing on Four-Year College Entry
While the NCES reports have some information about enrollment in less than four-year institutions, the focus is primarily on entry into four-year institutions. This approach tends to deemphasize the fact that over 40 percent of all first-time freshmen in degree-granting institutions enroll in a community college (National Center for Education Statistics, 2002). Some of these students go on to enroll in a four-year institution and attain a bachelor's degree. Understanding the role of family income, academic preparation, and the other factors that influence college participation is equally important for these students and for these institutions throughout the nation.

This issue is particularly critical since community colleges are an important entry point into postsecondary education for low-income youth. McPherson and Schapiro (1998) analyzed data from the 1994 American Freshman Survey of the UCLA Higher Education Research Institute to determine the enrollment of students from different income groups across higher education sectors. While 31 percent of all full-time freshmen were enrolled in community colleges,[22] 47 percent of freshmen from the lowest income group (family income of less than $20,000 in 1994) were enrolled in this sector (Table 5.1). In contrast, fewer than 14 percent of students from families making over $100,000 were in community colleges. Thus, by focusing on four-year college entry as an outcome, the NCES reports pay little attention to the experiences of many low-income students who see community college as the only postsecondary option available to them.

The Statistical Approach of the NCES Multivariate Analyses
     As described earlier, three of the Reports (1, 3, and 4) present multivariate analyses of the impact of several factors on college entry or persistence. Each report includes different sets of independent variables as predictors of the outcome of entry or persistence. Report 1 has the most parsimonious model; it includes only race, family income, parental education, college qualification index, and the two steps toward four-year college as predictors. The analyses in the other two reports include a broader set of variables as predictors.

     The NCES reports provide little information about some characteristics of these statistical models. For example, no measures of model fit, or the explanatory value of the models, are provided. Without these measures, it is impossible to tell how much of the variation in the outcome (college entry or persistence) is predicted by the independent variables, and thus, it is difficult to tell if the independent variables taken together are important predictors or have very little impact on the outcome.

     The reports also provide only final versions of the regression models and do not provide intermediate models that show the joint effects of conceptually grouped sets of predictors. In reporting multivariate results, it is a common convention to provide individual models that show the results of these groups of predictors on the outcome, building from a model with only one set of predictors up to a fully-specified model. In the models in these reports, such an approach would entail showing first, for example, the effect of student background characteristics, such as race, gender, family income, and parental education, on college participation. The next model would then add to these background traits the students' academic characteristics, such as the measures that make up the college qualification index, and show how the statistical fit or predictive value of this second model was improved over the first. This process would continue until all the variables were included in a fully-specified model. A process like this would provide the reader a sense of the importance of each group of variables in predicting the outcome.

     Related to this point is the minimal information provided in the reports explaining why certain variables were included or excluded from the multivariate models. It is impossible to tell why the model in Report 1 included only the five variables described above, while excluding any of the other variables available in the NELS survey shown by other research to be related to college entry. These were, in fact, reported on in the tabular analyses of that report. As noted earlier, the report did explain that financial aid variables were not included in the analysis because financial aid data were not available for students who did not enroll in college. However, inclusion of information about financial aid and the cost of college could provide valuable information about the choice of institutions for students who did enroll. For example, it might show whether students who received financial aid were more likely to attend a four-year institution than a community college.

Report 1 has a section of tabular analyses, described earlier, on the relationship between a number of background characteristics and the concern over college finances. That section of the report also explores similar relationships between students' background characteristics and steps taken to obtain information about financing a college education. It would be logical to ask whether these financial concerns, or the steps taken to obtain information about college financing, were predictors of college entry after controlling for other factors or vice-versa. Yet these variables were excluded from the multivariate analysis, and the authors provide no rationale for this decision.

As described earlier, the multivariate analysis of three-year persistence rates in Report 4 included no information about college costs and financial aid, other than the receipt of a Pell Grant, even though detailed information is available in the BPS Longitudinal Study. Given the existing research that has documented the effects of college prices and financial aid on the persistence of low-income students, it is unclear why the authors chose to exclude these variables from their analysis.

The final issue related to the statistical approach used in the NCES multivariate analyses is the problem of collinearity, also known as multicollinearity, or the correlation between the independent variables in the models. When independent variables are highly correlated, or statistically related to one another, the coefficients of the resulting model may be misestimated.[23] Researchers normally take steps to minimize the impact of collinearity on models by first measuring the correlation between independent variables. When two or more of these variables are highly correlated, standard procedure calls for one or more of them to be excluded from the model.[24] Failure to correct for collinearity may lead to a bias in the parameter estimates for the collinear variables. A common result of collinearity is to bias downward the estimates of the coefficients of correlated variables, thus leading one to conclude that a variable is not as important in predicting the outcome as it truly is.[25]

The NCES reports do not provide a correlation matrix of the variables used in the multivariate models, so it is impossible to gauge the exact impact that collinearity may have on the multivariate models. However, information provided in the NCES tabular analyses indicates that there may be a high degree of correlation between at least some of the predictors used in the models. For example, Table 1 of Report 1 shows that there appears to be a strong correlation between the key background characteristics used in the multivariate models in Reports 1, 3, and 4. While 52 percent and 54 percent of the Hispanic and black 1992 high school graduates, respectively, were from low-income families, only 34 percent of Asian/Pacific Islanders and 21 percent of whites were from this same group. Similarly, the nature of the relationship between family income and parental education can be seen in Figure 4.

Figure 4. Relationship Between Family Income and Parental Education, 1992 High School Graduates.

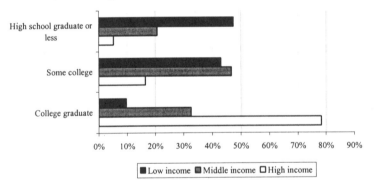

Source: Report 1, Table 1

While almost half of low-income students had parents who had never attended college, only five percent of high-income students were in this category. At the other end of the parental education scale, only ten percent of low-income students had at least one parent who graduated from college, while over three-quarters of high-income students were the children of college graduates.

Without analyzing the NELS data to measure the extent of the statistical correlation between these variables, it is impossible to determine the impact of collinearity on the multivariate analyses conducted by NCES. However, the relationships between some of the predictors that are demonstrated in the tabular analyses appear strong enough to question whether the results of the multivariate models may be biased by the effects of collinearity. One questionable result is that the parameter estimates of one or more of the correlated variables (for example race, family income, and parental education) may be biased downward, i.e., the statistical relationship between the outcome (college entry or persistence) and the predictor may actually be stronger than that reported by NCES.

The Impact of the Conflict Between the NCES Tabular and Multivariate Analyses

A key difference between the findings in the NCES tabular and multivariate analyses is in the relationship between family income and college participation. As noted in section three of this report, the NCES tabular analyses found that while 37 percent of low-income students had not enrolled in any form of postsecondary education within two years of high school graduation, only 21 percent of middle-income students and 7 percent of high-income students had not entered higher education within that same time period. In the NCES multivariate analyses, however, these differences were greatly reduced or even eliminated (see Figure 2).

The impact of this conflict between the tabular and multivariate results, as well as others that have been described in this report, is summarized in Table 5. Shown are the conclusions from the tabular analyses, how each issue is dealt with in the multivariate analyses, the statistical problem with this treatment, and the resulting contradictory conclusion.

Table 5.   Contradictions Between NCES Tabular and Multivariate Analyses.

Conclusion From Tabular Analyses	Treatment in Multivariate Analyses	Related Statistical Issue	Resulting Contradictory Conclusion
Financial barriers are important determinants of college enrollment for low-income students	Exclude college costs, financial aid, and unmet need as predictors and/or covariates	Omitted variable bias	Financial barriers are not important determinants of enrollment for low-income students
Access to college is unequal among low-, middle-, and high-income students	Focus exclusively on use of college-qualification index, as well as requirement of taking SAT/ACT tests and applying to four-year institution	Selection bias	There are small, if any, differences in college access for students who are college-qualified and take necessary steps toward enrollment
Finances discourage low-income, college-qualified high school graduates from taking the necessary steps toward enrollment	Ignore the effects of finances on steps toward enrollment, and include the steps as independent variables	Endogeneity bias	Taking steps toward enrollment enables low-income students to attend college at the same rates or close to those of their high-income peers
Family income is a major barrier to access and persistence for high school graduates	Attribute the joint effects of family income and parental education to parental education alone	Collinearity	Parental education is the major barrier to access and persistence for high school graduates

It cannot be known from the information presented in the NCES reports whether correcting the methodological problems outlined in Table 5 would resolve the contradictory results between the tabular and multivariate analyses. However, until the methodological problems are addressed, it is misleading to accept the conclusions of the reports that develop from the multivariate analyses.

Conclusions and Recommendations for Further Research

The four NCES reports reviewed in this study provide valuable information regarding the relationships between a number of variables and college participation in this country. However, because of the limitations of some of the data sets used, along with some decisions by NCES and its contractors regarding the focus of the reports, the four provide very limited information about the impact of college costs and financial aid on college participation.

The four reports require very careful readings by experienced researchers to understand the complex nature of these relationships. In an attempt to simplify the presentation of the results and keep the details of the analyses to a minimum, the reports may lead to a misinterpretation of some key findings. Given the importance and visibility of the work of NCES in informing postsecondary education policy throughout the country and, particularly, in light of the reauthorization of the HEA that will be taken up by Congress and the Administration this year, it is critical that the work of NCES achieve the highest standards of research.

The policy implications of the methodological problems outlined in this study should not be overlooked. For example, the conclusion in the NCES reports that differences in college-going rates are largely attributable to differences in parental education levels, rather than income, could lead to the conclusion that there is little that federal or state governments, or institutions can do to help close the gap in college participation between rich and poor. Levels of parental educational attainment are largely immutable, at least in the short run. However, if the differences in college entry rates are at least in part a factor of differences in resources among these groups—a conclusion that is not just plausible, but likely given the findings of other researchers—then there *is* a role for government and higher education institutions in closing the gap. The policy levers of financial aid and tuition levels can be utilized to help overcome these differences in resources.

There are a number of actions that NCES or other researchers, provided they are given access to the data used by NCES, can take to add to our understanding of the dynamics of college entry and persistence presented in these four reports. One step is to provide more details of the process followed in conducting the existing multivariate analyses, as described in the previous section of this study. This additional information would allow researchers to gauge the statistical validity of the analyses conducted by NCES, and thus provide more evidence of the value these models may have for informing higher education policy and practice. These should include:

1. More information about the statistical fit of the models;
2. Presentation of the intermediate models leading up to the fully-specified models shown in the existing reports; and
3. More information about the correlation of predictor variables and the tests for and potential effects of collinearity in the multivariate models.

A second action that could be undertaken by NCES would be to perform a reanalysis of the existing data to include variables in the multivariate models that were excluded in the initial work. These variables should be included based on the conceptual and empirical work conducted by other researchers that has explored the relationship between different factors and the outcomes of college entry and persistence. The NCES researchers should provide a thorough explanation of the rationale for including or excluding each variable. In particular, the researchers should consider the inclusion of more variables related to financial aid and college costs.

A third area of study is for NCES to examine its use of the college qualification index and the additional two steps toward entry described as taking the SAT or ACT and applying to college. As described earlier, such an approach introduces the issue of selectivity bias into the analyses and does not account for the impact of college prices and financial aid on the decisions of students to make themselves "college-qualified." At a minimum, NCES should present the same type of tabular analyses found in Report 1, which focus almost exclusively on college-qualified students, for those students who were not college-qualified. Since low-income students are disproportionately found in this latter group, more information should be provided about their pre-collegiate experiences.[26]

A fourth area for reexamination is the focus on the experiences of students entering four-year institutions, and the steps taken by students to qualify themselves for entry into these institutions. As noted earlier, over 40 percent of all first-time freshmen are enrolled in community colleges. Understanding more about the predictors of entry into these institutions could help inform policy.

Finally, NCES should analyze the need for a new nationally representative longitudinal study of high school graduates. Such a study should combine the detailed data about the high school and in some cases, middle school experiences found in NELS, with the postsecondary information found in the NPSAS. The strength of NELS is that it includes data from surveys of students, as well as their teachers, parents, and school administrators. It also includes high school transcript data and the administration of aptitude tests to the respondents. The NPSAS surveys contain detailed information from student interviews, as well as student-record data from the students' postsecondary institutions.

The NELS cohort of high school graduates is already over ten years old. Much has changed in both secondary and postsecondary education in the last decade, and in both public and institutional policy. A new longitudinal survey that combines the level of detail found in NELS and NPSAS would provide valuable data for researchers to answer many of the questions regarding the impact of financial aid and college costs on college participation, questions that NCES has had difficulty answering given the limitations of the existing data sets and the focus chosen by NCES in these reports.

This additional research would help to expand our existing knowledge base, and would allow scholars and policymakers to have a better understanding of the relationship between financial aid and college participation.

Notes

1. This chapter has been adopted from an earlier study conducted for the Advisory Committee on Student Financial Assistance (Heller, 2003).
2. Some of this loan and work study aid goes to graduate students; the focus of this chapter is solely on college participation by undergraduate students.
3. The four reports are described in section three of this chapter.
4. A high school diploma or GED is the minimal credential required for entry into most postsecondary education institutions.
5. These figures represent the proportion of each group enrolled in college, using the average for the years from 1997 to 2000.
6. See for example Levy and Murnane (1992) and Mortenson (1995, 1999a).
7. It also should be noted here that Kane conducted these analyses with and without controlling for the educational level of the student's parents. In both methods family income was still a large indicator of whether the student would enroll in college, even among these most academically-talented students.
8. While each report was written by contractors, rather than NCES staff, because of the oversight role of NCES they are being referred to here as "NCES reports."
9. Because Reports 1 and 3 analyze data from students who graduated high school in 1992, the analyses there are restricted to dependent students, often labeled "traditional college students." Report 4 includes all beginning students, dependent and independent alike.
10. The percentages across the three reports varied slightly (less than one percentage point in each category), due most likely to slight differences in the samples of students included in the analysis.
11. Report 2 is primarily a summary of other NCES analyses, and thus, does not present original analyses of its own.
12. These reports measure parental education as the highest level achieved by either parent or guardian of the student.
13. Because Reports 1 and 3 did not include multivariate analysis of entry into *any* form of postsecondary education, we cannot tell the impact of family income on this outcome.
14. This same table presents the counter-intuitive finding described earlier that students whose parents had some college experience, but no bachelor's degree, had persistence rates that

were *below* those of students whose parents had no college, thus further calling into question the value of parental education in predicting college persistence.

15.   The phrases "financial aid" and "college costs" are used here broadly to include such measures as tuition prices, cost of attendance, net prices, effective family contribution, and unmet need.

16.   This analysis does not include those students who had not graduated from high school by 1992.   Because low-income students are more likely to drop out of high school, they would be disproportionately excluded before the point at which this analysis was conducted.

17.   Report 1 does not mention in the highlights section that the college entry rates of low-income students still lagged behind those of their high-income peers by ten percentage points, controlling for other factors (table 34).

18.   This is reinforced by the fact that students and parents tend to *overestimate* the cost of college, and the overestimation tends to be greatest among low-income families (Ikenberry & Hartle, 1998; National Center for Education Statistics, 2001).

19.   See for example Hossler, Schmit, & Vesper (1999) and McDonough (1997).

20.   While measures of some of these assistance factors are available in the NELS survey, they evidently were not included in the multivariate analyses in Report 1.

21.   It should be noted here that the contractors hired to write the NCES reports are generally prohibited from discussing the policy implications of their findings in those reports.

22.   This proportion is less than that reported by NCES because the American Freshman Survey includes only full-time students, while the NCES figures include all students in community colleges.

23.   See Kennedy (1992) and Kleinbaum, Kupper, and Muller (1988) for more on the problems of collinearity in multivariate models.

24.   Another alternative is to combine the correlated variables into a "composite" variable, similar to what NCES has done in creating the college qualification index.

25.   A related problem is that of endogeneity, where predictor variables are related to one another though not linearly correlated. Endogeneity can result in a similar downward bias in the coefficient estimates.   The NCES reports do not provide the information

necessary to judge the degree that endogeneity may be affecting the results of the multivariate analyses.

26.   Report 3 does provide more information about all high school graduates, not just those who were college qualified, but its scope is more limited than Report 1.

References

Behrman, J. R., Kletzer, L. G., McPherson, M. S., & Schapiro, M. O. (1992). *The college investment decision: Direct and indirect effects of family background on choice of postsecondary enrollment and quality* (DP-18). Williamstown, MA: Williams Project on the Economics of Higher Education.

Berkner, L. (1998). *Student financing of undergraduate education: 1995-96* (NCES 98-076). Washington, DC: U.S. Department of Education, National Center for Education Statistics.

Berkner, L., Berker, A., Rooney, K., & Peter, K. (2002). *Student financing of undergraduate education: 1999-2000* (NCES 2002-167). Washington, DC: U.S. Department of Education, National Center for Education Statistics.

Clotfelter, C. T. (1991). Financial aid and public policy. In C. T. Clotfelter, R. G. Ehrenberg, M. Getz, & J. J. Siegfried (Eds.), *Economic challenges in higher education* (pp. 89-123). Chicago: University of Chicago Press.

Ellwood, D. T., & Kane, T. J. (2000). Who is getting a college education? Family background and the growing gaps in enrollment. In S. Danziger & J. Waldfogel (Eds.), *Securing the future: Investing in children from birth to college* (pp. 283-324). New York: Russell Sage Foundation.

Heller, D. E. (in press). *Review of NCES research on financial aid and college participation.* Washington, DC: U.S. Department of Education, Advisory Committee on Student Financial Assistance.

Heller, D. E. (1997). Student price response in higher education: An update to Leslie and Brinkman. *Journal of Higher Education, 68*(6), 624-659.

Heller, D. E. (1999). Racial equity in college participation: African American students in the United States. *Review of African American Education, 1*(1), 5-29.

Hossler, D., Schmit, J., & Vesper, N. (1999). *Going to college: How social, economic, and educational factors influence the decisions students make.* Baltimore, MD: The Johns Hopkins University Press.

Ikenberry, S. O., & Hartle, T. W. (1998). *Too little knowledge is a dangerous thing: What the public thinks about paying for college.* Washington, DC: American Council on Education.

Jackson, G. A. (1989). *Responses of black, Hispanic, and white students to financial aid: College entry among recent high school graduates.* College Park, MD: National Center for Postsecondary Governance & Finance, U. of Maryland.

Jackson, G. A., & Weathersby, G. B. (1975). Individual demand for higher education. *Journal of Higher Education, 46*(6), 623-652.

Kane, T. (1999). *The price of admission: Rethinking how Americans pay for college.* Washington, DC: Brookings Institution Press.

Kennedy, P. (1992). *A guide to econometrics.* Cambridge, MA: The MIT Press.

Kleinbaum, D. G., Kupper, L. L., & Muller, K. E. (1988). *Applied regression analysis and other multivariate methods* (2nd ed.). Boston: PWS-KENT Publishing Company.

Koretz, D. (1990). *Trends in the postsecondary enrollment of minorities.* Santa Monica, CA: The RAND Corporation.

Leslie, L. L., & Brinkman, P. T. (1988). *The economic value of higher education.* New York: American Council on Education/Macmillan Publishing.

Levy, F., & Murnane, R. J. (1992). U.S. earnings levels and earnings inequality: A review of recent trends and proposed explanations. *Journal of Economic Literature, 30,* 1333-1381.

Manski, C., & Wise, D. (1983). *College choice in America.* Cambridge, MA: Harvard University Press.

McDonough, P. M. (1997). *Choosing colleges: How social class and schools structure opportunity.* Albany: State University of New York Press.

McPherson, M. S., & Schapiro, M. O. (1998). *The student aid game: Meeting need and rewarding talent in American higher education.* Princeton, NJ: Princeton University Press.

Morey, L. (1928). Student fees in state colleges and universities, *School and Society, 28* (712), 185-192.

Mortenson, T. (1995). Educational attainment by family income 1970 to 1994. *Postsecondary Education OPPORTUNITY, 41,* 1-8.

Mortenson, T. G. (1999a). Family income by educational attainment 1956-1997. *Postsecondary Education OPPORTUNITY, 82,* 11-16.

Mortenson, T. G. (1999b). Parental educational attainment and higher educational opportunity. *Postsecondary Education OPPORTUNITY, 79,* 1-14.

Mortenson, T. G. (2001a). College participation by family income, gender and race-ethnicity for dependent 18 to 24 year olds 1996 to 2000. *Postsecondary Education OPPORTUNITY, 114,* 1-8.

Mortenson, T. G. (2001b). Family income and higher education opportunity 1970 to 2000. *Postsecondary Education OPPORTUNITY, 112,* 1-9.

National Center for Education Statistics. (2001). *The condition of education 2001* (NCES 2001-072). Washington, DC: U.S. Department of Education.

National Center for Education Statistics. (2002). *Digest of education statistics, 2001.* Washington, DC: U.S. Department of Education.

President's Commission on Higher Education. (1947) *Higher Education for American Democracy.* New York: Harper & Brothers.

Rooney, C., & Schaeffer, B. (1998). *Test scores do not equal merit: Enhancing equity & excellence in college admissions by deemphasizing SAT and ACT results.* Cambridge, MA: National Center for Fair & Open Testing.

Rouse, C. E. (1994). What to do after high school: The two-year versus four-year college enrollment decision. In R. G. Ehrenberg (Ed.), *Contemporary policy issues in education* (pp. 59-88). Ithaca, NY: ILR Press.

St. John, E. P. (1990). Price response in persistence decisions: An analysis of the high school and beyond sophomore cohort. *Research in Higher Education, 31*(4), 387-403.

St. John, E. P. (1991). What really influences minority attendance? Sequential analyses of the High School and Beyond sophomore cohort. *Research in Higher Education, 32*(2), 141-158.

Tuma, J., & Geis, S. (1995). *Student financing of undergraduate education, 1992-93* (NCES 95-202). Washington, DC: U.S. Department of Education, National Center for Education Statistics.

United States Bureau of the Census. (2001). *School enrollment in the United States—Social and economic characteristics of students* (P20-533). Washington, DC: Author.

CHAPTER 3

OMITTED VARIABLES AND SAMPLE SELECTION IN STUDIES OF COLLEGE-GOING DECISIONS[1]

William E. Becker

Introduction

USA Today (September 17, 2003) had headlines saying "Most high school grads don't have what it takes for college: Only 32% of 18-year-olds met criteria for readiness; minorities fared worst." The article reports on a study of college-going behavior done under the auspices of the Manhattan Institute by Greene and Forster (2003). It quotes Greene saying that figures show virtually all of the minority college-ready students actually do attend college, suggesting that financial aid and affirmative action policies may not affect the number of minority students in college. Theirs is but one more study employing faulty methods and reaching the similarly erroneous conclusions advanced by four earlier studies commissioned by the National Center for Education Statistics (NCES) on the determinants of initial college enrollment and persistence toward a baccalaureate degree: Berkner and Chavez (1997), Choy (2001), Horn and Nuñez (2000), and Wei and Horn (2002).

In essence, the authors of the NCES multivariate analyses and those that followed give the impression that family income, college costs or the availability of financial aid are not important in the college-going decisions of students. As pointed out by Heller (2003), the current wave of studies gives the impression that the

65

paramount variable in the college-going decision is being college-qualified (according to the NCES studies, that is, completed relatively rigorous academic high school courses, achieved sufficient grades/class rank, took the SAT/ACT, and applied to college).

This chapter extends the work of Heller (2003) by providing an econometric assessment of the consequences of omitting relevant financial variables from a multivariate analysis of college-going decisions, ignoring the sample selection issues and related endogeneity issues associated with focusing only on those who are college-qualified, and not adequately considering the implications of highly related variables that are believed to influence college enrollment and persistence decisions. Also provided are suggestions and examples of how the data should be re-analyzed to provide consistent estimators of the relevant parameters in student-choice models of the college-going decision.

Before addressing the technical issues associated with omitting relevant financial variables from an assessment of the college-going decision and focusing only on those who are college-qualified and associated endogeneity problems, it may be helpful to consider an analogy involving a contest of skill between two types of contestants: Type A and Type B. There are 8 of each type who compete against each other in the first round of matches. The 8 winners of the first set of matches compete against each other in a second round, and the 4 winners of that round compete in a third. Type A and Type B may compete against their own type in any match after the first round, but one Type A and one Type B manage to make it to the final round. In the final match they tie. Should we conclude, on probabilistic grounds, that Type A and Type B contestants are equally skilled? How is your answer affected if I tell you that on the first round 5 Type As and only 3 Types Bs won their matches and only the one Type B was successful in the second and third round? This additional information should make clear that we have to consider how the individual matches are connected and not just look at the last match. But before you conclude that Type As had a superior attribute only in the early contests and not in the finals, consider another analogy provided by Thomas Kane.[2]

Kane has a hypothetical series of races between 8 greyhounds and 8 dachshunds. In the first race, the greyhounds enjoy a clear advantage with 5 greyhounds and only 3 dachshunds finishing among the front-runners. These 8 dogs then move to the second race, when only one dachshund wins. This dachshund survives to the final race when it ties with a greyhound. Kane asks: "Should I conclude that leg length was a disadvantage in the first two races but not in the third?" And answers: "That would be absurd. The little dachshund that made it into the third race and eventually tied for the win most probably had an advantage on other traits—such as a strong heart, or an extraordinary competitive spirit—which were sufficient to overcome the disadvantage created by its short stature."

These analogies demonstrate all three sources of bias found in the NCES's recent studies of college-going and persistence decisions: sample selection bias, endogeneity, and omitted variables. For example, the length of the dogs' legs not appearing to be a problem in the final race (financial aid not appearing important among those who jump the hurdles to become college-qualified) reflects the sample selection issues resulting if the researcher only looked at that last race. Looking only at the last race (corresponding to those who apply to college) would be legitimate if the races were independent (high school and college educational decisions were independent), but they are sequentially dependent; thus, the endogeneity problem. As Kane points out, concluding that leg length (income/expense variables) was important in the first two races (high school) and not in the third (going to college) reveals the omitted-variable problem: a trait such as heart strength or competitive motivation (known availability of financial aid) might be overriding short legs and thus should be included as a relevant explanatory variable in the analyses. The mathematics of selection, endogeneity and relevant omitted variables are well known, and they are the focus of my chapter.

A Primer on Omitted Relevant Variables and Related Problems

Reports by Berkner and Chavez (1997) and Horn and Nuñez (2000) focus on enrollment in college within two years of high school graduation as the outcome, whereas the report by Wei and Horn (2002) focuses on continuous enrollment in college through 1998 for those students who began in the 1995-1996 academic year. The report by Choy (2001) is a summary of other studies. Heller notes that family income and parental education appear as explanatory variables in all of the studies. Either because of the lack of data (in the National Education Longitudinal Study) or explicit omission, however, only the multivariate analysis of persistence by Wei and Horn (whose work included low- and middle-income students) made any attempt to include financial data in the explanation of the college decision.[3] But even in the work of Wei and Horn, whether the student received a Pell Grant or not in the first year of college was the only financial variable used as a regressor (other than family income). There were no other financial variables (for tuition, cost of attendance, net price, loans, state grants, institutional grants, or the like) included.

The omission of financial data other than family income renders these NCES studies suspect in ways even more severe than those recognized by Heller. From the early work of Griliches (1957) and Theil (1957), the consequence of omitting relevant explanatory variables has been well known. The bias that results from excluding an explanatory variable with available or unavailable data can be seen in the bivariate choice to enroll in college. The ith potential student's decision to enroll in college ($Y_i = 1$) or not enroll ($Y_i = 0$) can be related to sets of variables represented in two matrices: $\mathbf{X}_{1i}$ and $\mathbf{X}_{2i}$, where the subscript i indicates the ith student's record in the ith row of the two matrices. The first matrix, $\mathbf{X}_{1i}$, contains a column of ones and sets of explanatory variables related to the student's characteristics (SAT/ACT score, grade point average/class rank, etc.), family characteristics (parent income, education, etc.), environmental factors (peers, social category, etc.). The second matrix, $\mathbf{X}_{2i}$, contains the financial variables related to college cost (tuition, cost of attendance, loans, state grants, institutional grants, etc.). The linear probability model is then written:

$$Y_i = \mathbf{X}_{1i}\boldsymbol{\beta}_1 + \mathbf{X}_{2i}\boldsymbol{\beta}_2 + \varepsilon_i \qquad (1)$$

where $\boldsymbol{\beta}_1$ and $\boldsymbol{\beta}_2$ are vectors of parameters to be estimated that correspond to the variables in the $\mathbf{X}_1$ and $\mathbf{X}_2$ matrices. Each of the epsilon error terms ε_i in the vector of error terms ε is assumed to have an expected value (mean) of zero and be unrelated to the variables in $\mathbf{X} = \mathbf{X}_1 + \mathbf{X}_2$; i.e., $E(\varepsilon \mid \mathbf{X}) = 0$ and $E(\mathbf{X}'\varepsilon) = 0$. Thus,

$$E(Y_i \mid \mathbf{X}_i) = \mathbf{X}_{1i}\boldsymbol{\beta}_1 + \mathbf{X}_{2i}\boldsymbol{\beta}_2 = \mathrm{Prob}(Y_i = 1) \qquad (2)$$

because

$$E(Y_i) = (1)[\text{Prob}(Y_i = 1)] + (0)[1 - \text{Prob}(Y_i = 1)] = \text{Prob}(Y_i = 1).$$

Although the error terms in the linear probability model are distributed as binomial random variables and do not have constant variance, as required for hypothesis testing with ordinary least squares estimators of the β coefficients, the coefficients in the $\boldsymbol{\beta}_1$ and $\boldsymbol{\beta}_2$ vectors can be estimated without bias if both $\mathbf{X}_1$ and $\mathbf{X}_2$ are included.[4] But if the college financial variables in $\mathbf{X}_2$ are omitted ($Y_i = \mathbf{X}_{1i}\boldsymbol{\beta}_1 + \varepsilon_i^r$), then the expected value of the ordinary least squares estimator $\mathbf{b}_1^r$ of the $\boldsymbol{\beta}_1$ vector is:

$$E(\mathbf{b}_1^r) = \boldsymbol{\beta}_1 + [\mathbf{X}_1'\mathbf{X}_1]^{-1}\mathbf{X}_1'\mathbf{X}_2\boldsymbol{\beta}_2 \qquad (3)$$

The second term in equation (3) shows that unless all of the parameters in $\boldsymbol{\beta}_2$ are zero, or $\mathbf{X}_1$ and $\mathbf{X}_2$ are orthogonal (unrelated regressors), the parameters in the $\boldsymbol{\beta}_1$ vector are estimated with bias by $\mathbf{b}_1^r$. That is, $E(\mathbf{b}_1^r) = \boldsymbol{\beta}_1$ only if $\boldsymbol{\beta}_2 = 0$ or $\mathbf{X}_1'\mathbf{X}_2 = 0$; or in English, the bias depends on the values of the omitted variables, given the included variables, and the parameters of the omitted variables.

Because this point will be critical when we consider the maximum-likelihood estimators of probit and logit index models of college enrollment, the bias or lack of bias in the ordinary least squares estimation $\mathbf{b}_1^r$ does not depend on the distribution of epsilon. It only depends on $\boldsymbol{\beta}_2$ and $\mathbf{X}_1'\mathbf{X}_2$. This may be easier to appreciate by considering a simple case of two explanatory variables: say parental income (which we will label x_1) from the larger data set in matrix $\mathbf{X}_1$ and financial aid (labeled x_2) from the larger omitted data set in matrix $\mathbf{X}_2$[5] That is, as in equation (1), the true linear probability model is now:

$$Y_i = \beta_0 + \beta_1 x_{1i} + \beta_2 x_{2i} + \varepsilon_i \qquad (4)$$

with critical error term assumptions $E(\varepsilon_i \mid x_{1i}, x_{2i}) = 0$ and $E(\varepsilon_i x_{ji}) = 0$. Financial aid is dependent on family income. Let this relationship be given by:

$$x_{2i} = \delta_0 + \delta_1 x_{1i} + \eta_i \qquad (5)$$

where the δ's are parameters and η_i is the well-behaved error term associated with the ith student's financial aid—that is, its mean is zero, $E(\eta_i \mid x_{1i}) = 0$; it has constant variance, $E(\eta_i^2 \mid x_{1i}) = \sigma_\eta^2$; and it is not related to x_1, $E(x_{1i}\eta_i) = 0$. But if the college financial variable x_2 is omitted ($Y_i = \beta_0 + \beta_1 x_{1i} + \varepsilon_i^r$), then the expected value of the income coefficient estimator b_1^r is

$$E(b_1^r) = \beta_1 + \delta_1\beta_2 \qquad (6)$$

If family income and financial aid are not related ($\delta_1 = 0$), then b_1^r is an unbiased estimator of the family income effect on college enrollment, even though the financial aid variable was omitted. But if family income and financial aid are negatively related ($\delta_1 < 0$), then b_1^r is a biased estimator of the family income effect on college enrollment when the financial aid variable is omitted. In particular, if family income and financial aid are negatively related, excluding the financial aid variable from the college-going decision implies that the effect of family income is underestimated.

In the case of enrollment decisions, all the financial aid variables that enter into the "net price" for a college education (which are excluded from the four NCES studies) are clearly related to parental income and other explanatory variables included in the explanation of the college-going decisions in matrix $\mathbf{X}_1$. Thus, the parameters estimated in these studies are biased. In particular, to the extent that the excluded financial variables are negatively (positively) correlated with the included variable, the estimated coefficients can be expected to under-(over-)estimate the parameters of the included variables.

Worth noting is that the inclusion of parental income, parental education, and college financial variables (e.g., net price) in an equation aimed at explaining the college-going decision may make it difficult to estimate the individual effect of these variables, as Heller mentions in his review, because these variables can be highly related. This problem of multicollinearity, however, does not justify excluding some of these variables from the regression. Omitting them implies that correlation has just been built into the error term and the included regressors, because the effect of the excluded variable(s) is relegated to the error term.[6] When included regressors are highly correlated little can be done to untangle the detrimental effects on estimated coefficient standard errors without new sample data or outside information that can be used to drive the determinant of the $\mathbf{X'X}$ away from zero or otherwise affect the variance covariance matrix. As suggested by Heller, to assess the influence of multicollinearity reporting pair-wise correlations or other measures of regressor dependence might be helpful. One might also consider conducting an F test for sets of coefficients of potential explanatory variables that are suspected of being highly collinear and ignoring individual t statistics.[7]

Omitted variables are not the only source of regressor and error term correlation. Including regressors that are jointly dependent with the variable to be explained (endogeneity) is another source. For example, in the NCES study by Berkner and Chavez (1997), attending a college is made a function of being "college-qualified," with this designation used as a zero-one covariate in their two- and four-year college enrollment regressions. But the factors that go into planning to attend college are the same factors that enter the decision to become college-qualified; thus, becoming college-qualified is said to be endogenous in an explanation of the decision to attend college—it is not an independent explanatory variable—it is at least in part determined along with the amount of education to be pursued.

There are several ways in which the designate "college-qualified" can be shown to be endogenous. For example, as recognized by the NCES researchers, becoming college-qualified is itself a function of many factors, which the NCES researchers arbitrarily restrict to completing relatively rigorous academic high school courses, achieving sufficient grades/class rank, taking the SAT/ACT, and applying to college. Instead of this subjective definition of being college-qualified, the full set of factors that determine whether the ith student is truly college-qualified can be written as:

$$(collegequalified)_i = f_i(many\ factors) + \varphi_i \qquad (7)$$

where φ_i is the error term reflecting the uncertainty in the ith student's qualification, and the enrollment (Y_i), again written for simplicity as a linear probability model, is:

$$Y_i = \beta f_i(many\ factors) + ... + \varepsilon_i \qquad (8)$$

But, as in the Berkner and Chavez regression, if enrollment is specified as:

$$Y_i = \beta(collegequalified)_i + ... + \varepsilon_i\ * \qquad (9)$$

then $\varepsilon_i^* = \varepsilon_i - \beta\varphi_i$, by substituting equation (7) into equation (8). A positive shock to the error term φ_i in the college-qualified equation (7) produces a like positive move in being college-qualified in both equations (7) and (9) and a negative move in ε_i^*. Thus, "*college qualified*" and ε^* are related in equation (9); college-qualified is endogenous, and β would be estimated with bias.

Finally, although of no consequence in our discussion of multicollinearity and endogeneity, implicit in the linear probability model is a heterogeneity problem that is caused by the variance of ε_i depending on the values in the data matrix $\mathbf{X}_i$. This heterogeneity can be removed with a generalized least squares routine.[8] More critically, even though $E(Y_i \mid \mathbf{X}_i) = \text{Prob}(Y_i = 1)$ is between 0 and 1, there is no assurance that the predicted probability of college enrollment in a linear probability model will fall between 0 and 1. For this reason, the linear probability model is best viewed as a starting and comparison point for estimating the probability of enrolling in college. Because of its simplicity, it is ideal for showing the bias introduced to parameter estimation when omitted relevant variables are related to the included explanatory variables or problems of endogeneity are suspected.

Latent Regression, Logits and Probits, and Omitted Variables

Consider the student's decision to enroll in college. Classical microeconomic theory states that the student will enroll if the net utility or net benefit of enrolling is positive. It is intuitively appealing, although not necessary, to interpret this net utility as the unobservable latent variable y^*. For the ith student,

$$y_i^* = \mathbf{X}_i\boldsymbol{\beta} + \varepsilon_i \qquad (10)$$

where $\mathbf{X}$ is again the data matrix of explanatory variables of all students; $\boldsymbol{\beta}$ is the vector of related parameters; the error term vector is $\boldsymbol{\varepsilon}$; and the subscript i denotes the appropriate row for the ith student. The error term ε_i is again assumed to have a mean of zero. If a logit model is specified, then $y_i^* = \text{Ln}[\text{Prob}(Y_i = 1)/\text{Prob}(Y_i = 0)]$. If a standardized probit model is specified, then $y_i^* = -z_i$ (where z is a standard normal score from which probability is calculated) and ε_i has a variance of $\sigma_\varepsilon^2 = 1$. (With no loss in generality, the unit variance for ε_i is achieved by interpreting the beta coefficients as divided by the standard deviation of epsilon for scaling. This scaling issue becomes critical when the omitted-variable problem is considered in what follows.)

Both the logit and probit models ensure that the predicted probabilities of college enrollment lie between zero and one, but these models greatly increase the mathematical complexity of parameter estimation via maximum-likelihood, nonlinear-iterative routines that require a properly specified population model from which the data are believed to be generated. Other than for reasons of computation, which current computer programs handle with equal ease, there is typically little reason to prefer a probit or logit model. The main difference between probit and logit models is that the conditional probability of enrolling in college approaches the extreme values of zero or one at a slightly slower rate in a logit than in a probit because the logistic distribution has slightly fatter tails. The implications of omitted relevant explanatory variables on the consistent estimators of parameters (estimates that collapse on their true expected values of the betas as the sample size goes to infinity) are similar in the logit and probit models, but as we will see, different than in the linear probability model.

If the student enrolls in college, then we observe $Y_i = 1$ and infer that $y_i^* > 0$. If there is no college enrollment, then $Y_i = 0$ is observed and $y_i^* \leq 0$ is inferred. Making the distinction between the college financial variables $\mathbf{X}_2$ and the other columns in the data matrix $\mathbf{X}$ gives the basic college enrollment model as:

$$y_i^* = \mathbf{X}_{1i}\boldsymbol{\beta}_1 + \mathbf{X}_{2i}\boldsymbol{\beta}_2 + \varepsilon_i \tag{11}$$

$Y_i = 1$ (observed college enrollment), if $y_i^* > 0$ (unobserved)

$Y_i = 0$, if $y_i^* \leq 0$

For simplicity in algebra, and to make explicit the nature of the omitted variables problem in a latent regression model of binary choice, consider only a two explanatory variable model for the propensity to enroll in college:

$$y_i^* = \beta_0 + \beta_1 x_{1i} + \beta_2 x_{2i} + \varepsilon_i \tag{12}$$

$Y_i = 1$, if $y_i^* > 0$ and $Y_i = 0$, if $y_i^* \leq 0$

If x_2 and x_1 are related linearly as before in equation (5), then equation (12) can be rewritten as:

$$y_i^* = \beta_0 + \beta_1\delta_0 + (\beta_1 + \beta_2\delta_1)x_{1i} + \varepsilon_i + \beta_2\eta_i \qquad (13)$$

If ε and η are independently distributed as normal random variables, conditioning on x_1, then equation (13) is a bivariate probit model, where again $y_i^* > 0$ for $Y_i = 1$ and $y_i^* \le 0$ for $Y_i = 0$.

In the linear probability model, any bias in the estimation of the coefficients of the included variables depends on the values of the omitted variables, given the included variables, and the parameters of the omitted variables. Unlike this linear probability model, estimation of β_1 in a latent regression model depends on the assumed distribution of the error term $\varepsilon_i + \beta_2\eta_i$. There can be bias in the estimation of β_1 even if the excluded and included explanatory variables are unrelated because the iterative estimation process depends on the error term distribution (intuitively, think of it as drawing from the error term distribution to generate the unobserved y_i^* values). For the ith student in equation (13), the error term $\varepsilon_i + \beta_2\eta_i$ has a mean of zero and a variance of $\beta_2^2\sigma_\eta^2 + \sigma_\varepsilon^2$. Assuming the error term is a standard normal random variable for maximum-likelihood estimation of β_2 in the probit specification implies that β_2 is involved in the scaling of β_1. From Yatchew and Griliches (1985), we know that maximum-likelihood estimators of β_0 and β_1 converge to:

$$\frac{\beta_0 + \beta_2\delta_0}{\sqrt{\beta_2^2\sigma_\eta^2 + \sigma_\varepsilon^2}} \quad \text{and} \quad \frac{\beta_1 + \beta_2\delta_1}{\sqrt{\beta_2^2\sigma_\eta^2 + \sigma_\varepsilon^2}} \qquad (14)$$

From the second ratio in (14), omitting the financial aid variable x_2 from the estimation of the propensity to enroll in college, equation (12), has two effects on the estimation of family income coefficient β_1. First, as in the linear probability model, there is the bias in the family income coefficient that is equal to the coefficient of the omitted financial aid variable ($\beta_2 > 0$), times the coefficient of the income variable in the regression of the omitted financial variable on the included parent income variable ($\delta_1 < 0$). Second, and unlike the linear probability model, there is a rescaling effect determined by the standard deviation $\sqrt{\beta_2^2\sigma_\eta^2 + \sigma_\varepsilon^2}$ in the denominator of equation (14), which does not vanish even if there is no relationship between family income and financial aid ($\delta_1 = 0$). That is, omitted relevant variables in a probit model result in biased estimation of the coefficient of the included explanatory variables regardless of the relationship between the included and excluded variables.

Although individual coefficients cannot be estimated without bias when relevant variables are omitted from a probit model, relative effects can be estimated if the omitted variables are not correlated with the included variables.[9] For example, the estimate of the slope relative to the intercept is the ratio of the two ratios in (14), which is (β_1 / β_0), if β_2 is zero. Of course, if the omitted and included variables are related ($\beta_2 \neq 0$), then as in a nonlinear probability model individual and relative effects cannot be calculated without bias.

The omitted-variable problems found in the estimation of probit models also exist in other nonlinear probability models. In particular, excluding the financial variables from a logit model produces a bias in the maximum-likelihood parameter estimates for the included explanatory variables, regardless of the relationship among the included and excluded variables. From the early work of Lee (1982), the existence of this bias in the logit model has been known:

> In the standard linear (probability) model, if the omitted variable and the included variable are independent, the coefficient of the included variable will not be affected. But this is not so for the logit model. (p. 208)

Biased estimation of the coefficient of included explanatory variables in either a probit or logit model of enrollment will occur even if the included and excluded variables are independent.

Sample Selection

Berkner and Chavez (1997) and Horn and Nuñez (2000) provide multivariate analyses only for college-qualified students (i.e., those who have completed relatively rigorous academic high school courses, achieved sufficient grades/class rank, took the SAT/ACT, and applied to college) who desire to enroll and/or persist in college.

Family income and parental education level are explanatory variables considered in all four NCES reports. Other explanatory variables (such as race, gender, an index of "college qualification," educational expectations, and whether the student took a college entrance examination) appear in only one or two of the reports. As already addressed, one of the two college participation outcomes considered by the NCES is students' initial enrollment in college. The second outcome is whether the students persist to degree attainment. For pedagogical ease, in this section I now treat these as one observable outcome (y_i^p) generated by a continuous random variable that measures the amount of time the ith student invests or persists in college. For example, y_i^p could be measured by the number of terms completed, with 0 reflecting a young person who never attended college and an undefined upper limit. The problems associated with sample selection and endogeneity can be demonstrated, using a modified version of the presentation in Becker and Powers (2001), with the model:

$$y_i^p = \mathbf{X}_i \boldsymbol{\beta} + \varepsilon_i = \beta_1 + \sum_{j=2}^{k} \beta_j x_{ji} + \varepsilon_i \qquad (15)$$

where again $\mathbf{X}$ is the data set of explanatory variables, $\mathbf{X}_i$ is the row of x_{ji} values for the relevant variables believed to explain the ith student's decision to enroll in and continue in college, the β_j's are the associated slope coefficients in the vector $\boldsymbol{\beta}$, and ε_i is the individual random shock (caused by unknown events, for example) that affect the ith student's persistence. In empirical work, the exact nature of y_i^p is critical. For example, to model the truncation issues in the distribution of epsilon a Tobit model can be specified for y_i^p. As we have already seen, to explicitly model only the college-going decision as a "yes" or "no" choice, a logit or probit model can be specified. These refinements do not alter the basic issues regarding sample selection and endogeneity addressed in this section.

In accordance with the National Center for Education Statistics, let $T_i = 1$, if the ith student is "college-qualified" (i.e., completed relatively rigorous academic high school courses, achieved sufficient grades/class rank, took the SAT/ACT, applied to college), and let $T_i = 0$, if not. Assume that there is an unobservable continuous dependent variable T_i^* underlying the ith student's decision to jump the NCES hurdles to be labeled college-qualified. Call this latent variable T_i^* the student's propensity to be college-qualified.

For the population of N students, let $\mathbf{T}^*$ be the vector of all students' propensities to be college-qualified. Let $\mathbf{H}$ be the matrix of explanatory variables that are believed to drive these propensities, which includes directly observable things (e.g., parental income and parental education), expected values (expected college net cost and expected future earnings), attitude variables (personal motivation and risk aversion) and environmental items (peer pressure, counseling, family support). Let α be the vector of corresponding slope coefficients. The individual random shocks that affect each student's propensity to become qualified for college are contained in the error term vector ω. The ith student's propensity to become college-qualified can now be written:

$$T_i^* = \mathbf{H}_i\alpha + \omega_i \qquad (16)$$

where

$T_i = 1$, if $T_i^* > 0$, and student i is college-qualified, and

$T_i = 0$, if $T_i^* \leq 0$, and student i is not qualified.

For estimation purposes, the error term ω_i is assumed to be a standard normal random variable that is independently and identically distributed with the other students' error terms in the ω vector. As already discussed, this probit model for the propensity to be college-qualified can be estimated using the maximum-likelihood routine in programs such as LIMDEP or STATA.

Studies supported by the NCES and others are aimed at establishing the effect of variables believed to influence decisions related to attending and succeeding in college. The effect of not including students who have not completed academic high school courses, do not have sufficient grades or class rank, do not take the SAT/ACT, and do not apply to college ($T_i = 0$) and an adjustment for the resulting bias caused by excluding these students from the NCES studies of these college-related decisions can be illustrated with a two-equation model formed by the selection equation (16) and the ith student's persistence into and through college, persistence equation (15)[10]. Each of the disturbance terms, ε_i, equation (15), is assumed to be distributed bivariate normal with the corresponding disturbance term in the ω vector of the selection equation (16). Thus, for the ith student we have:

$$(\varepsilon_i, \omega_i) \sim \text{bivariate normal}\,(0,0,\sigma_\varepsilon,1,\rho) \qquad (17)$$

and for all perturbations in the two-equation system we have:

$$E(\varepsilon) = E(\omega) = \mathbf{0}, \ E(\varepsilon\varepsilon') = \sigma_\varepsilon^2 \mathbf{I}, \ E(\omega\omega') = \mathbf{I}, \text{ and } E(\varepsilon\omega') = \rho\sigma_\varepsilon \mathbf{I} \quad (18)$$

That is, the disturbances have zero means, unit variance, and no covariance among students, but there is covariance between selection in getting the college-qualified status and persistence into and through college for each student.

The difference in the functional forms of the selection equation (16) and the persistence equation (15) ensures the identification of equation (15) but ideally other restrictions would lend support to identification. Estimates of the parameters in equation (15) are desired, but the ith student's college persistence y_i is observed in the NCES studies for only the subset of students for whom $T_i = 1$. The regression for this censored sample of $n_{T=1}$ students is:

$$E(y_i^p \mid \mathbf{X}_i, T_i = 1) = \mathbf{X}_i\boldsymbol{\beta} + E(\varepsilon_i \mid T_i^* > 0); \ i = 1, 2, \dots n_{T=1}$$
$$\text{(for } n_{T=1} < N\text{)} \qquad\qquad (19)$$

Similar to omitting a relevant variable from a regression, selection bias is a problem because the magnitude of $E(\varepsilon_i \mid T_i^* > 0)$ varies across individuals and yet is not included in the estimation of equation (15). To the extent that ε_i and ω_i (and thus T_i^*) are related, the estimators are biased.

The persistence regression can be adjusted for those who elected never to become college-qualified in several ways. An early Heckman-type solution to the sample selection problem is to rewrite the omitted variable component of the regression so that the equation to be estimated is:

$$E(y_i^p \mid \mathbf{X}_i, T_i = 1) = \mathbf{X}_i\boldsymbol{\beta} + (\rho\sigma_\varepsilon)\lambda_i; \ i = 1, 2, \dots n_{T=1} \qquad (20)$$

where $\lambda_i = f(-T_i^*)/[1 - F(-T_i^*)]$, and $f(.)$ and $F(.)$ are the normal density and distribution functions. The inverse Mill's ratio (or hazard) λ_i is the standardized mean of the disturbance term ω_i, for the ith student who was college-qualified; it is close to zero only for those well above the $T = 1$ threshold. The values of λ are generated from the estimated probit selection equation (16) for all students. Each student in the persistence regression gets a calculated value λ_i, with the vector of these values serving as a shift variable in the persistence regression. The estimates of ρ, σ_ε, and all the other coefficients in equations (15) and (16) can be obtained simultaneously using the maximum-likelihood routine in LIMDEP.

The Heckman-type selection model represented by equations (15) and (16) makes clear the nature of the sample selection problem inherent in establishing determinants of the college-going decision. Estimation of the parameters in this model, however, requires cross-equation exclusion restrictions (variables that affect selection but not enrollment and persistence), differences in functional forms, and/or distributional assumptions for the error terms. Parameter estimates are typically sensitive to these model specifications.

Alternative nonparametric and semiparametric methods are being explored for assessing treatment effects in nonrandomized experiments (Heckman, 1990; Manski, 1990; and Newey et al., 1990) but these methods have been slow to catch on in education research. Exceptions, in the case of financial aid and the enrollment decision, are the works of Wilbert van der Klaauw and Thomas Kane. Van der Klaauw (2002) estimates the effect of financial aid on the enrollment decision of students admitted to a specific East Coast college, recognizing that this college's financial aid is endogenous because competing offers are unknown and thus by definition are omitted relevant explanatory variables in the enrollment decision of students considering this college.

The college investigated by van der Klaauw created a single continuous index of each student's initial financial aid potential (based on a SAT score and high school GPA) and then classified students into one of four aid level categories based on discrete cut points. The aid assignment rule depends at least in part on the value of a continuous variable relative to a given threshold in such a way that the corresponding probability of receiving aid (and the mean amount offered) is a discontinuous function of this continuous variable at the threshold cut point. A sample of individual students close to a cut point on either side can be treated as a random sample at the cut point because on average there really should be little difference between them (in terms of financial aid offers received from other colleges and other unknown variables). In the absence of the financial aid level under consideration, we should expect little difference in the college-going decision of those just above and just below the cut point. Similarly, if they were all given the financial aid, we should see little difference in outcomes, on average. To the extent that some actually get it and others do not, we have an interpretable treatment effect.

(Intuitively, this can be thought of as running a regression of enrollment on financial aid for those close to the cut point, with an adjustment for being in that position.) In his empirical work, van der Klaauw obtained credible estimates of the importance of the financial aid effect without having to rely on arbitrary cross-equation exclusion restrictions and functional form assumptions. His estimates suggest that an additional $1,000 in financial aid results in a 4 to 5 percentage point increase in the probability of the mean student attending this university.

Kane (2003) uses an identification strategy similar to van der Klaauw but does so for all those who applied for the Cal Grant Program to attend any college in California. Eligibility for the Cal Grant Program is subject to a minimum GPA and maximum family income and asset level. Like van der Klaauw, Kane exploits discontinuities on one dimension of eligibility for those who satisfy the other dimensions of eligibility. His results suggest that additional financial aid dollars have a large impact on students' decisions even when provided late in the schooling process: "Financial aid applicants were 4 to 6 percentage points more likely to enroll in college as a result of the receipt of a Cal Grant A award, even after they have already made the investment of filing a federal financial aid form and applied to college" (p. 26). For comparison purposes if nothing else, there is value in pursuing these alternative approaches to the sample selection and endogeneity issues that van der Klaauw and Kane recognize as intrinsic to the analyses of the college-going decision.

Conclusion

The four NCES reports considered here and reviewed by Heller (2003) are limited by some of the data sets employed and by some decisions that NCES and its contractors made about the importance of including financial aid variables that other researchers have found to influence college-going decisions. Unfortunately, other researchers are using faulty methods and reaching similar erroneous conclusions as those advanced by the NCES reports on the determinants of initial college enrollment and persistence toward a baccalaureate degree. The NCES should commission a complete reanalysis of the existing data to include financial variables in the multivariate models that were excluded in the initial work but which others have found to influence college-going decisions. A thorough explanation of the rationale for including or excluding each variable must be provided based on the existing literature.

In addition to addressing the omitted-variable problems, NCES must reexamine its use of the college qualification index (and the additional two steps toward entry into four-year institutions of taking the SAT or ACT and applying to college). Use of this index introduces a sample selection problem that cannot be overcome by simply adding more variables or more observations. The problem of sample selection in the college-going decision arises because youths who elect to pursue a certain high school experience are those who expect schooling to have a favorable outcome for them. If expected outcomes are related to observed ones, then the outcomes experienced by youth who choose to become college-qualified would differ from those that non-college-qualified youth would have experienced if they had become college-qualified. From the early work of Nobel laureate James Heckman (1979), this sample selection problem and methods of adjusting for it are well known and should not have been overlooked by the NCES. Furthermore, Dominitz and Manski (1996) and Betts (1993) document the fact that youth from low income families greatly underestimate the return to a college education and thus can be expected not to pursue the steps required to become college-qualified:

> One of the most interesting patterns is that students whose parents' income was less than $50,000 tended to make significantly lower estimates of earnings of college graduates . . .young people form beliefs about the returns to education by observing workers in their neighborhoods. To the extent that families segregate themselves by income, students in low-income neighborhoods should systematically underestimate the return to education. (Betts, 1993, p. 37)

We can only assume that low-income students likewise would underestimate the financial aid available to them if they were to start down the more rigorous college prep path and succeeded in becoming college-qualified.[11]

It is absolutely essential that the studies and findings advanced by the NCES not be based on methodologies that do not adequately control for the high school student's expectations of the net cost of college and future earnings. Without including relevant financial aid measures in studies of college access and without adequately controlling for sample selection in the college-going decision, conclusions based on regression analyses about the importance of other explanatory variables cannot be taken seriously.

Notes

1. An earlier version of this work was prepared for the U.S. Department of Education Advisory Committee on Student Financial Assistance (Order Number ED-03-PO-1414). It has been presented at Macalester College, St. Paul, Minnesota (June 12, 2003) and a conference on Evaluation Methods and Practices Appropriate for Faith-Based and Other Providers of Social Service, Indiana University (October 3, 2003). In its preparation, extensive use was made of Chapters 17, 21, and 22 of William H. Greene, *Econometric Analysis,* 5th ed. (Prentice Hall, 2003). Personal communication with Greene on technical issues related to the nature of the omitted-variable problem in nonlinear probability models is gratefully acknowledged. Likewise, communication with Wilbert van der Klaauw on the use of nonparametric and semiparametric estimation of financial-aid effects is gratefully acknowledged. Suzanne Becker, William Goggin, Donald Heller, Michael McPherson, Edward St. John, John Siegfried, and Michael Watts are thanked for their critical reading of earlier versions.
2. Kane's example is from a letter sent to Jacqueline King (June 13, 2002) at the American Council on Education and reproduced here with his permission (April 14, 2003, email).
3. Edward St. John (2002) may have been the first education researcher to call attention to the NCES studies ignoring the effect of financial-aid variables when analyzing the cause of disparity in college access.
4. Because the error terms in a linear probability model are heteroskedastic, are not distributed normally, and predicted probabilities can lie outside the 0-1 interval, use of this specification is criticized other than for preliminary investigation and comparison purposes. Caudill (1988), however, argues that the linear probability model has an advantage over the probit and logit models when all members of a subgroup have the same outcome. For example, we may be interested in the effect of having completed high school calculus on the college-going

decision. If every student who took high school calculus went to college, the coefficient on the high school calculus dummy is not estimable in either a logit or probit model, but it can be estimated in a linear probability model. Heckman and Snyder (1997) provide a general derivation for the linear probability model as a representation of a random utility model.

5. The financial aid variables are typically treated as exogenous in single equation enrollment models. Without adequate control variables included in the regression, this is a dubious assumption.

6. The building of a model based on data-mining routines such as stepwise regression is doomed by the omitted variable problem. If a relevant variable is omitted from a regression in an early step, and if it is related to the included variables then the contribution of the included variables is estimated with bias. It does not matter with which of the related explanatory variables you start; the contribution of the included variables will always be biased by the excluded.

7. The null hypothesis that a financial aid variable (or sets of variables) has no effect can never be accepted for there is always another hypothesized value, in the direction of the alternative hypothesis, that cannot be rejected with the same sample data and level of significance. The Type II error inherent in accepting the null hypothesis is well known but often ignored by researchers.

8. In the linear probability model heteroskedasticity of the error term does not lead to inconsistent estimation of the regression parameters, but the standard errors will be wrong (inconsistently estimated). That is why heteroskedasticity-corrected standard errors must be reported.

9. In semiparametric estimation of the discrete choice models, as seen in Klein and Spady (1993), the inability to identify the intercept is common. In those papers the focus is only on the relative parameter values.

10. Although y_i^p is treated as a continuous variable this is not essential. For example, a bivariate choice (probit or logit) model can be specified to explicitly model only the college-going decision as a "yes" or "no" for students who enrolled within two years of high school graduation as in L. Berkner and L. Chavez, "Access to Postsecondary Education for the 1992 High School Graduates" (NCES 1997, 98-105) and L. Horn and A.-M. Nuñez, "Mapping the Road to College: First-Generation Students' Math Track, Planning Strategies and Context Support (NCES 2000 2000-153). The selection issue is then modeled in a way similar to

that employed by Boyes, Hoffman and Low (1989) regarding loan defaults given the granting of a loan and Greene (1992) on consumer loan default and credit card expenditures. The two-equation model for the ith student enrolling given he or she is college-qualified is then based on:

y_i^p = 1, if student actually enrolled in a college, and 0 otherwise.
T_i^i = 1, if student is college-qualified, and 0 otherwise.

As with the standard Heckman selection model, this two-equation system involving bivariate choice and selection can be estimated in a program like LIMDEP.
11. Linsenmeier, Rosen, and Rouse (2003) report in a study based on a single institution that substituting grants for loans did not have a significant effect on the likelihood that low-income students actually start college at the school making the switch. However, the switch did have a larger effect on minorities than other like low-income students, suggesting that minority students' expectations of their post-college income are less certain, giving a bigger impact to the importance of the financial-aid mix.

References

Becker, W. E., & Powers, J. (2001). Student performance, attrition, and class size given missing student data. *Economics of Education Review, 20* (August), 377-388.

Berkner, L., & Chavez, L. (1997). *Access to postsecondary education for the 1992 high school graduates* (NCES 98-105).

Betts, J. R. (1996). What do students know about wages? *Journal of Human Resources, 31* (1), 27-56.

Boyes, W., Hoffman, D., & Low, S. (1989). An econometric analysis of the bank credit scoring problem. *Journal of Econometrics, 40* (1), 3-14.

Caudill, S. B. (1988). An advantage of the linear probability model over probit and logit. *Oxford Bulletin of Economics and Statistics, 50* (4), 425-427.

Choy, S. P. (2001). *Students whose parents did not go to college: Postsecondary access, persistence, and attainment* (NCES 2001-126).

Dominitz, J., & Manski, C. F. (1996). Eliciting student expectations of the returns to schooling. *Journal of Human Resources, 31* (1), 1-26.

Greene, J. P. & Forster, G. 2003. Public high school graduation and college readiness rates in the United States. Manhattan Institute for Policy Research. http://www.manhattan-institute.org/html/ewp_03.htm

Greene, W. H. (1992). *A statistical model for credit scoring.* Department of Economics, Stern School of Business, New York University, September 29.

Griliches, Z. (1957). Specification bias in estimates of production functions. *Journal of Farm Economics, 39* (1), 8-20.

Heckman, J. (1979). Sample bias as a specification error. *Econometrica, 47* (1), 153-161.

Heckman, J. (1990). Varieties of selection bias. *American Economic Review, 80* (May), 313-318.

Heckman, J., & Snyder, J. M. (1997). Linear probability models of the demand for attributes with an empirical application to estimating the preferences of legislators. *Rand Journal of Economics, 28* (special issue), S142-S189.

Heller, D. E. (2003). *Review of NCES research on financial aid and college participation.* Report prepared for the Advisory Committee on Student Financial Assistance. Draft: March.

Horn, L., & Nuñez, A.-M. (2000). *Mapping the road to college: First-generation students' math track, planning strategies, and context of support* (NCES 2000-153).

Kane, T. (2003). A quasi-experimental estimate of the impact of financial aid on college-going. NBER Working Paper No. W9703 May.

Klein, R. & Spady, R. (1993). An efficient semiparametric estimator for discrete choice models. *Econometrica, 61* (2), 387-421.

Lee, L. (1982). Specification error in multinomial logit models: Analysis of the omitted variable bias. *Journal of Econometrics, 20* (2), 197-209.

Linsenmeier, D., Rosen, H., & Rouse, C. (2003). Financial aid packages and college enrollment decisions: An econometric case study. National Bureau of Economic Research, Working Paper No. 9228.

Manski, C. (1990). Nonparametric bounds for treatment effects. *American Economic Review, 80* (May), 319-323.

Newey, W., Powell, J. & Walker, J. (1990). Semiparametric estimation of selection models: Some empirical results. *American Economic Review, 80* (May), 324-328.

86

St. John, E. P. (2002). The access challenge: Rethinking the causes of the new inequality. Policy Issue Report #2002-1. Bloomington, IN: Indiana Education Policy Center, School of Education.

Theil, H. (1957). Specification errors and the estimation of economic relationships. *Review of the International Statistical Institute, 25* (1/3), 41-51.

van der Klaauw, W. (2002). Estimating the effect of financial aid offers on college enrollment: A regression-discounting approach. *International Economic Review,* (November), 1249-1288.

Wei, C. C., & Horn, L. (2002). *Persistence and attainment of beginning students with Pell Grants* (NCES 2002-169).

Yatchew, A., & Griliches, Z. (1985). Specification error in probit models. *Review of Economics and Statistics, 67* (1), 134-139.

CHAPTER 4

ACCESS REVISITED: A PRELIMINARY
REANALYSIS OF NELS

John B. Lee

The central problem in education is the stubborn persistence of educational inequality. The correlation of income, race, and ethnicity with educational achievement continues despite aggressive attempts to equalize educational opportunity, enrich educational offerings, and provide financial support to help low-income students pay for college.

This chapter looks at the two main constraints on access to college—money and academic preparation—and makes some recommendations regarding how federal dollars can be spent to maximize the enrollment of low-income students in college. The problem is that there is a high degree of relationship between the two measures. Lower-income students are more likely to have inadequate academic preparation than are higher-income students. Solving the problem is important because education provides a foundation for a better economic life. This promise is especially important for low-income students. Income disparities are growing in the U.S. Between the late 1980s and the late 1990s, the real income of the lowest-income families grew by an insignificant 1 percent after a decade of decline. The real income of middle-income families grew by 2 percent; the average income of high-income families grew by 15 percent (Bernstein, McNichol, Mishel, & Zahradnik, 2000). The result of this trend is that a college degree has become more important economically.

& Zahradnik, 2000). The result of this trend is that a college degree has become more important economically.

Methodology and Data

The National Educational Longitudinal Study (NELS) of 1988 was used for most of the tables in this report. NELS is a product of the National Center for Education Statistics in the U.S. Department of Education. It provides a nationally representative sample of eighth-graders taken in the spring of 1988. A sample of these respondents was then resurveyed through four follow-ups in 1990, 1992, 1994, and 2000. Students reported on school, work, and home experiences, as well as educational resources and support. In addition, the data include information on parents and peers, neighborhood characteristics, educational and occupational aspirations, and student perceptions. The dataset includes achievement test scores in reading, social studies, mathematics, and science.

Students' teachers, parents, and school administrators were also surveyed. Coursework and grades from students' high school and postsecondary transcripts are available. The resulting data allow us to evaluate the influence of family background, academic preparation, and economic measures on college attendance patterns.

The data was used to calculate two measures of academic preparation. The first estimate is for high school students who took at least algebra II and received a diploma (no GED or certificates of completion). This represents minimal preparation for college. It is assumed that if a high school student took at least second-year algebra, he or she probably had at least begun a college preparatory program.

The second set of academic criteria represents a more rigorous measure, including a mix of characteristics typical of four-year college students. It includes the following measures:

1. Rank in the 54th percentile in high school,
2. Having an academic GPA of at least 2.7,
3. A combined SAT/ACT score of 820/19,
4. A NELS math and reading score at the 56th percentile.

These criteria do not include direct measures of academic content, but provide a set of indicators that track with high school curriculum.

We used enrollment within one year of graduating from high school as a measure of college enrollment. We did not include enrollment in subassociate degree vocational institutions in the analysis. High school graduates were divided into socio-economic quartiles. This is a derived variable that includes family income, parents' level of education, and job status[1]. The analysis only examines younger students as they graduate from high school, so it does not include the full range of students that enroll in higher education.

The chapter provides a preliminary reanalysis of NELS using definitions of college qualification similar to the ones used by NCES. As others indicate (Becker, Chapter 3; Heller, Chapter 2), further reanalysis is needed.

What is the Evidence?

The distribution of 1992 high school graduates who met the minimum standard of academic preparation for college is illustrated in Figure 1. The figure makes two related points. First, the number of high school graduates who are minimally qualified for college declines by SES. Second, more than twice as many of the high SES high school graduates were minimally qualified for college when they finished high school than were those in the lowest quartile.

Figure 1. Number of High School Graduates Who Are Minimally Qualified for College, by SES Quartile.

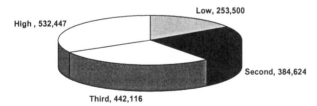

Source: NELS: 88-00

The percent of minimally qualified students who enrolled in college within one year of graduating from high school is illustrated in Figure 2. The figure shows the increasing enrollment in college by each higher-SES group, and the increasing share of students in each SES quartile that enrolls in four-year institutions.

Forty-five percent of the low SES students who were minimally qualified for college enrolled in college somewhere compared with 84 percent of those from the high SES.

Figure 2. Percent of Qualified High SES Graduates Enrolling in a 2- or 3-Year Institution.

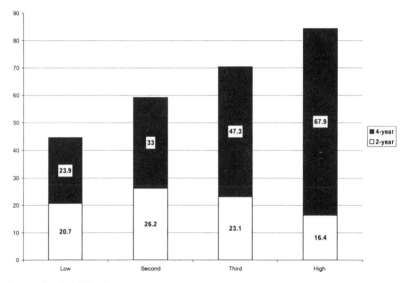

Source: NELS: 88-00

The fact that fewer low SES students met the minimum qualification to attend college and a smaller percent of them enrolled leads to the conclusion that very few low SES students start college. Nearly four times as many high school graduates in 1992 who were in the highest SES quartile entered college than did from the lowest SES (see Figure 3).

Figure 3. Number of Students Enrolling in College, by SES Quartile.

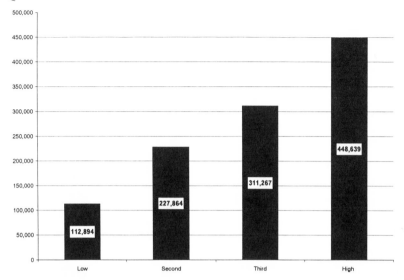

Source: NELS: 88-00

As shown in Figure 1, 253,500 low SES students graduated from high school with at least minimal academic preparation to go to college and 112,894 went to college. That leaves over 140,000 low SES students who could have gone to college, but did not.

Using the more rigorous academic criteria sharpens the differences among SES quartiles in the number of high school students who met the minimum levels of academic qualification to attend a four-year college (Figure 4).

Compared with the first standard, over 92,000 fewer students in the low SES quartile met this standard. Just over 28,500 of the students in the high SES quartile that met the first standard did not meet this standard. This supports the conclusion that high school students in the highest SES quartile were better prepared academically when they graduated than were those in the lowest SES.

Figure 4. Number of Students Meeting More Rigorous Standard of Academic Preparation, by SES Quartile.

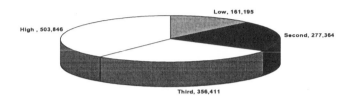

Source: NELS: 88-00

Figure 5. Percent of Students Who Met Rigorous College Preparation Criteria, Who Enrolled in Two- and Four-year Colleges, by SES.

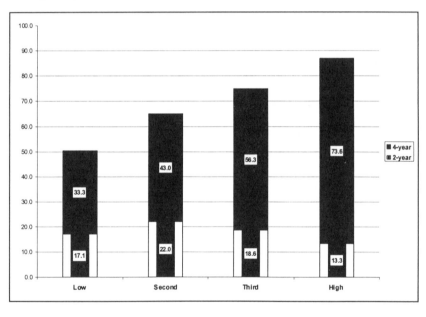

Even with the more rigorous academic standard, high school graduates from the lowest SES were still less likely to go to college than those in the highest quartile (Figure 5). Roughly half of the lowest SES high school graduates who met the academic criteria went on to college within the first year after finishing high school. That compares with 87 percent of the students from the highest SES quartile. The results show that something other than ability or academic preparation keeps students from enrolling in college, especially those from the lowest SES quartile.

Finances

The total amount contributed by families and students at different levels of expected family contribution (EFC) is documented in Figure 6. EFC is a proxy for income and represents the amount of money that colleges expect families to contribute. It is calculated by a formula that takes income, family size, number in college, assets, and extraordinary expenses into consideration to determine the amount that a family should have available to help pay for education.   The amount of aid is an actual number provided in the National Postsecondary Student Aid Study (NPSAS: 00) for students enrolled in colleges that cost between $10,700 and $11,700 in 1999-2000. This is the price of attending a four-year public college and living on campus.

The results show that the lowest-income students attending these schools had less than half the money it took to attend (Figure 6). Generally, families in this lowest EFC group make less than $25,000 annually. The total money available to students does not equal the cost of attendance until family EFC approaches $7,500.

This gap between the amount the student has available from all sources and the price of attendance represents a looming gap that might dissuade a student from applying or reduce his or her willingness to enroll full-time. It might even dissuade a high school student who was academically qualified from considering college.

The difference between price and resources must be made up by working. A single dependent student in the lowest-income group would have to make at least $6,000 a year after taxes just to pay the additional college costs not covered by student aid.

Figure 6. Student Budget of $10,700-$11,700, NPSAS 99-00.

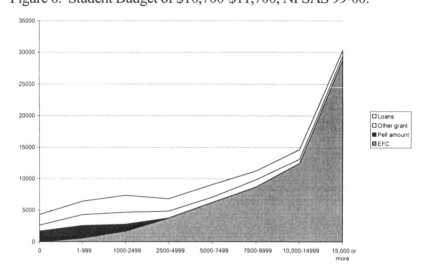

Source: NPSAS: 00

At the current minimum wage of $5.15 per hour, a student would have to work 1,200 hours a year (.15 an hour for withholding) to earn enough to attend college. That represents 23 hours a week every week of the year. This is at the upper limit of working for a full-time student. Low-income students are faced with two alternatives—work too much or attend college part-time. Both of these events are associated with not graduating.

What is the Future?

The prospects for getting more aid to low-income students are not great. In 2000-01, the maximum Pell Grant covered 42 percent of the fixed cost of attendance at four-year public colleges. Even with a dramatic increase in appropriations in recent years, the Pell Grant has half the purchasing power it did two decades ago. Without increasing the appropriations for the program at a much higher rate than has been realized in the past, the purchasing power of the Pell Grant will continue to shrink, leaving low-income students further behind in their ability to afford college.

Enrollments will probably increase by 10 percent over the next decade. This is a conservative estimate, half of the 20 percent projected by NCES in 2001. That will require an increase of between 10 percent and 20 percent in Pell appropriations over the decade to keep up with growing enrollment. Over the last decade, the price of attendance has been increasing at about 4 percent annually and has been matched by increases in Pell appropriations. The more successful we are in getting low-income students to attend college, the more we will increase demand for Pell Grants.

If the past predicts the future, the next decade will see an erosion of 1 to 2 percent a year in Pell Grant purchasing power. This projection assumes no change in eligibility, no influx of low-income students, and no expansion of eligibility.

Conclusions

In recent years, Congress and the states have addressed the issue of affordability by providing more financial aid to middle-income students in the form of grants—often with a merit component—loans, and tax subsidies. This represents a political judgment, not an analytical judgment about where public money will do the most good. Economists have argued against this policy because price of attendance is not as much of a consideration for middle-income families as it is for low-income families. A bedrock assumption that justifies the award of student aid is that low-income students are more sensitive to the price of attendance and the availability of student aid than are higher-income students (Kane, 1999). Simply stated, as the price of attendance increases and financial aid is in short supply, low-income students will not attend college, but higher-income students will.

The Pell Grant continues to be the cornerstone of federal support for low-income students. Even with recent increases, the Pell Grant falls far short of providing enough support to allow a low-income student to attend a four-year college and live on campus without depending too much on work.

Unless Congress increases appropriations well above the 4 percent annual rate of recent years, the Pell Grant will continue to shrink as a share of college price over the next ten years. We need an increase in appropriations of 10 percent annually for a decade to reach the point that the average award would cover half the cost of attending a public college full-time.

The main reason for emphasizing improvement in aid to low-income students instead of improving academic preparation is that we do not seem to know how to make systematic improvements in academic preparation. The Pell Grant appropriation is something Congress can control.

The National Assessment of Educational Progress shows relatively little change in reading, mathematics, and science scores for 17-year-old students since 1969 (Phillips, 1999). Academic preparation is the responsibility of local schools and states. The federal government can provide help to local schools, but cannot directly improve education. This is another reason to suggest that the most efficient way to improve enrollment of low-income students in college is to increase the amount of grant aid available to those low-income students who have met the academic standards set by colleges and the states.

The prospect is that the financial problems for low-income students will get progressively worse unless Pell Grant appropriations increase faster than inflation. The combination of an increasing college-age population and inflation in the price of attendance over the next decade will require significant increases in support of low-income students just to allow them to stay.

Notes

1.   All variable definitions came from the Data Analysis System, or DAS, available on the Web (http://nces.ed.gov/das/).

References

Bernstein, J., McNichol, E.C., Mishel, L., & Zahradnik, R. (2000). *Pulling apart: A state by state analysis of income trends.* Washington, DC: Center on Budget and Policy Priorities, Economic Policy Institute.

College Board. (2002). *Trends in student aid.* Washington, DC: Author.

Kane, T. J. (1999). *The price of admission.* Washington, DC: Brookings Institution Press.

SECTION II

The State Role

CHAPTER 5

STATE MERIT SCHOLARSHIP PROGRAMS

Donald E. Heller[1]

Introduction

Publicly funded scholarships in the United States, since they began in significant levels in the 1960s, have been awarded primarily based on the financial need of the student and his or her family, with the goal of increasing access to college and eliminating disparities in college participation among students from different socioeconomic groups. Beginning with passage of the *Higher Education Act of 1965*, and in particular, establishment of Basic Educational Opportunity Grants (now called Pell Grants) in the *Education Amendments of 1972*, federally funded student aid has been used in order to help achieve equality of postsecondary educational opportunity (Mumper, 1996). The State Student Incentive Grant program, also part of the Title IV student-aid programs, encouraged the development of state-funded scholarships. Many states responded by creating programs that used financial need as the primary criterion for awarding grants. The basic goal was to permit families to have access and choice for college in spite of their income levels.

Financial aid is particularly critical for meeting the college access needs of minority students in the United States. Recent data from the United States Bureau of the Census (2002) indicate that in 2000, the median income of white families with at least one child ($60,226) was almost twice that of black ($30,841) and

Hispanic ($33,288) families. Because of these differences in family resources, minority students depend much more upon financial aid to be able to afford a college education.

Comparing State Scholarship Programs

State-funded grants have become an increasingly important source of financial aid in the last two decades. From the 1980-81 academic year to 2001-02, current dollar spending on federal Pell and Supplemental Educational Opportunity Grants increased 286 percent (College Board, 2002), while spending on state-sponsored grants to undergraduates increased 499 percent (National Association of State Scholarship and Grant Programs, various years).

During this period, however, the use of financial need as the main basis for awarding scholarships by the states has eroded. Academic merit—measured in many different forms—has replaced financial need as the primary determinant for the awarding of scholarships in most of the new state grant programs developed over the last decade.[2] Between 1991 and 2001, spending by the states on need-based scholarships for undergraduates increased 7.8 percent annually, while spending on merit programs increased at a 20.1 percent annual rate (National Association of State Scholarship and Grant Programs, various years). The proportion of state grants awarded based on merit, rather than need, has risen from 10 percent to 24 percent during this period.

The first and best known broad-based state merit scholarship program is the Helping Outstanding Pupils Educationally (HOPE) program in Georgia. Begun in 1993, it is now the largest state-run merit scholarship program in the country, awarding approximately $350 million in 2001-02. Funded by the Georgia Lottery, the program awards scholarships to students who attain a B average in high school core curriculum subjects (Mumper, 1999). Students have to maintain a B average while enrolled in college in order to retain the scholarship. The scholarship provides for full tuition (plus a $150 per semester book allowance) at any public institution in the state, or $3,000 for students attending a private institution in the state. While the program originally included a family income cap of $66,000, by its third year the cap had been removed.

The popularity of Georgia HOPE helped spur the development of similar programs in other states. As of 2002, 12 states had implemented broad-based merit scholarship programs that do not use financial need in determining eligibility.[3] These states awarded over $1 billion in merit awards during the 2001-02 academic year, three times the $339 million provided in need-based aid by those states (National Association of State Student Grant & Aid Programs, 2003). Table 1 summarizes these programs.

As the table indicates, many of the programs share some common characteristics, but there are important differences. Florida's Bright Futures Scholarship program, like Georgia's, uses the state lottery as a funding source and awards full scholarships to students attending state-sponsored institutions of higher education (and a comparable amount to those enrolled in private institutions). But the criteria for the scholarships in Florida include SAT scores as well as grade point averages, while Georgia relies only on grade point averages.

Michigan's Merit Award Scholarship, meanwhile, awards one-time grants of $2,500 to students attending state-sponsored institutions who earn high scores on the state's curriculum-based assessment. The program is funded by the state's share of the national tobacco settlement.

New Mexico's Success Scholarship is similar to Georgia's, in that it awards full scholarships to students who attend state-sponsored colleges and universities and is funded by the state lottery. But the criterion for awarding Success Scholarships is first-year college grade point averages.

States have articulated three primary motivations for the creation of these programs:

- To promote college access and attainment. The Michigan law that established that state's award program, for example, stated as a goal that the program would "increase access to postsecondary education" (Michigan Merit Award Scholarship Act, 1999).
- To encourage and/or reward students who work hard academically. The Florida statute creating its program states that it was created "to reward any Florida high school graduate who merits recognition of high academic achievement" (Florida Bright Futures

Table 1. State Merit Scholarship Programs

Program (year implemented)	Funding Source	Award Criteria	Award Amount
Alaska Scholars Award (1999)	Land leases and sales	Class rank	$2,750 per year at the University of Alaska
Florida Bright Futures Scholarship	Lottery	GPA and SAT/ACT	Up to full tuition and fees at a FL public institution plus $300, or a comparable amount at a FL private institution
Georgia Helping Outstanding Pupils Educationally (HOPE) Scholarship (1993)**	Lottery	GPA	Full tuition and fees at a GA public institution, or up to $3000 at a GA private institution
Kentucky Educational Excellence Scholarship (1999)	Lottery	GPA	Up to $1000 per year at a KY public or private institution
Louisiana Tuition Opportunity Program for Students (1998)	General revenues	GPA and ACT	Full tuition and fees at a LA public institution, or a comparable amount at a LA private institution
Michigan Merit Award Scholarship (2000*)	Tobacco settlement	State curricular framework test	One-time award up to $2500 at a MI public or private institution; $1000 out-of-state
Mississippi Eminent Scholars Program (1996)	General revenues	GPA and SAT/ACT	$2500 at a MS public or private institution
Missouri Higher Education Academic Scholarship Program ("Bright Flight") (1997)	General revenues	SAT/ACT	$2000 at a MO public or private institution

Program (year implemented)	Funding Source	Award Criteria	Award Amount
Nevada Millennium Scholarship (2000)	Tobacco settlement	GPA	$80 per credit hour at a NV four-year public or private institution or $40/$60 per credit hour (lower division) at a NV community college
New Mexico Lottery Success Scholarship (1997)***	Lottery	GPA	Full tuition and fees at a NM public institution
South Carolina Legislative for Future Excellence (LIFE) Scholarship	General revenues	GPA, SAT/ACT, and class rank	Full tuition plus $300 at a public SC institution; comparable amount at a SC private institution
West Virginia Providing Real Opportunities for Maximizing In-State Student Excellence (PROMISE) Scholarship (2002)	Lottery and taxes on amusement devices	GPA, SAT/ACT	Full tuition at a WV public institution or comparable amount at a WV private institution

* See Chapter 2 for more about this program. ** See Chapters 4, 5, and 6 for more about this program. *** See Chapter 3 for more about this program.
Sources: Krueger (2001), Selingo (2001), and state program Web sites.

Scholarship Program, 1997). The Web site for West Virginia's PROMISE scholarship, meanwhile, cites other states' experience as evidence that the program has a motivational effect: "Several other states have found that the quickest and most effective way to motivate students to study harder and to achieve in school is to offer good students the opportunity to attend college tuition free" (Promise Scholarship Program, 2002).

• To stanch the "brain drain" of the best and brightest students and encourage them to attend college in the state. As the University of Alaska web site states, "The

UA Scholars Program is designed to help reduce the number of Alaska's high school graduates who leave the state for education and jobs elsewhere" (University of Alaska, 2002).

Promotional material for South Carolina's LIFE Scholarship, meanwhile, claims all three goals: "The purpose of the LIFE Scholarship program is to increase access to higher education; improve employability of South Carolina's students; provide incentives for students to be better prepared for college; and to encourage students to graduate from college on time" (South Carolina Commission on Higher Education, 2002).

Research on more traditional need-based grant programs has demonstrated their effectiveness in promoting college access, particularly for lower-income students.[4] Recent research on these newer, merit scholarship programs, however, demonstrates that they do little to promote college access and educational attainment in a state. A recent report from the Civil Rights Project at Harvard University examined four of the nation's largest state merit aid programs in Florida, Georgia, Michigan, and New Mexico (Heller & Marin, 2002). The findings in this report are very consistent. Using different data as well as varying research methodologies, the authors find that state merit scholarships are being awarded disproportionately to populations of students who historically, and today, have the highest college participation rates. This includes students from middle- and upper-income families, as well as white students.[5] The authors of the studies in that report conclude that rather than helping to move each state closer to the goal of equality of educational opportunity, these merit scholarship programs are likely to exacerbate existing gaps in college participation, causing poor and minority students to fall further behind their wealthier and white peers.

Conclusion

The question of the effectiveness of different forms of financial aid in promoting college access is crucial at a time when postsecondary access has become a critical public policy issue in the country. In particular, policy makers are growing concerned about the persistent gaps in postsecondary participation between rich and poor, and between racial majority and minority students (Advisory Committee on Student Financial Assistance, 2001).

These gaps have persisted despite the implementation of need-based and merit-based aid; for example, the gap in college participation rates between students in the lowest-income quartile and those in the highest-income quartile is almost as large today as it was 30 years ago, before implementation of Pell Grants and the state grant programs described in this chapter.

While many issues influence whether students attend college—including academic preparation, family and peer influences, and sociocultural factors—financial resources play an important part in contributing to the participation rate gap. According to *Access Denied*, the report of the Advisory Committee on Student Financial Assistance (2001) lower-income students face a staggering amount of unmet need—the difference between the cost of attending college and the amount of funds available from a student and her family's resources, including all forms and sources of financial aid—compared with their more affluent peers. In 1996, the report notes, lower-income students attending four-year public institutions faced an average unmet need of $3,800 per year, compared to $400 for higher-income students. Thus, the typical lower-income student would face a total unmet need in excess of $15,000 if they were able to attain a baccalaureate degree in just four years, a daunting task today for even the most well-prepared and well-financed student. At community colleges, unmet need averaged $3,200 per year for lower-income students, compared to $100 for wealthier students. If state scholarships are unable to narrow these gaps, or at least not exacerbate them, the challenge of increasing access to higher education for low-income students will be severe.

Understanding the impact of merit scholarship programs is particularly important in light of the challenges facing higher education in the near future. Research conducted by Carnevale and Fry (2002) shows that higher education is likely to face an increase in enrollments of 1.6 million undergraduates in the next dozen years. In addition, the income and racial profile of this influx of students indicates that the need for grants and scholarships to help pay for college will grow faster than the growth in enrollment, putting even more demands on financial aid resources.

At the same time the nation is facing these demographic trends, state capacity for funding higher education—along with the willingness to do so—is being diminished. A report produced by the National Center for Public Policy and Higher Education outlined the constrained revenue growth faced by the states, combined with the increased need for funding areas other than higher education (Hovey, 1999). More recent trends indicate that the fiscal picture is unlikely to brighten in the near future. For the 2003-04 academic year, half of the states reduced their appropriations to higher education institutions, with the average cut by approximately five percent (Potter, 2003). These fiscal constraints will only make it more difficult for states to meet the financial needs of the coming cohorts of students.

The trends in state financial aid and appropriations do not bode well for the efforts to achieve equality of postsecondary educational opportunity. If progress is to be made, states must recommit to focusing on meeting the needs of underrepresented students in higher education.

Notes

1.   The author acknowledges the research assistance of Roger Geertz Gonzalez and Kimberly Rogers on portions of this article.
2.   Many states have small, non-need aid programs targeted at specific populations (such as military veterans, dependents of state employees, or widows and orphans of police or fire personnel killed in the line of duty). The programs described in this report include those programs that are generally available to any resident of the state who meets the specified merit criteria. Three additional states (California, Arkansas, and Washington) have broad-based merit programs that do utilize a family income cap.
3.   Ohio has a program that awards $2,100 scholarships per year based on high school GPA and ACT score, but the program is restricted to a maximum of only 1,000 awards statewide. Thus, it is not considered a broad-based program as described here.
4.   See Heller (1997), Jackson and Weathersby (1975), and Leslie and Brinkman (1987) for reviews of the literature on tuition prices, financial aid, and college access.
5.   This chapter is based on the introduction to that report and is reprinted with permission of the Civil Rights Project.

References

Advisory Committee on Student Financial Assistance. (2001). *Access denied: Restoring the nation's commitment to equal educational opportunity.* Washington, DC: U.S. Department of Education.

Carnevale, A. P., & Fry, R. A. (2002). The demographic window of opportunity: College access and diversity in the new century. In D. E. Heller (Ed.), *Condition of access: Higher education for lower income students* (pp. 137-151). Westport, CT: Greenwood Publishing Group (ACE/Praeger Series on Higher Education).

College Board. (2001-2). *Trends in student aid, 2002.* Washington, DC: Author.

Florida Bright Futures Scholarship Program, Florida Statutes, 240.40201 §10 (1997).

Heller, D. E. (1997). Student price response in higher education: An update to Leslie and Brinkman. *Journal of Higher Education, 68*(6), 624-659.

Heller, D. E., & Marin, P. (2002). *Who should we help? The negative social consequences of merit scholarships.* Cambridge, MA: The Civil Rights Project, Harvard University.

Hovey, H. A. (1999). *State spending for higher education in the next decade: The battle to sustain current support.* San Jose, CA: National Center for Public Policy and Higher Education.

Jackson, G. A., & Weathersby, G. B. (1975). Individual demand for higher education. *Journal of Higher Education, 46*(6), 623-652.

Krueger, C. (2001). *Merit scholarships.* Denver, CO: Education Commission of the States.

Leslie, L. L., & Brinkman, P. T. (1987). Student price response in higher education. *Journal of Higher Education, 58*(2), 181-204.

Michigan merit award scholarship act, 390.1451 (1999).

Mumper, M. (1996). *Removing college price barriers: What government has done and why it hasn't worked.* Albany: State University of New York Press.

Mumper, M. (1999, November). *HOPE and its critics: Sorting out the competing claims about Georgia's HOPE scholarship.* Paper presented at the annual meeting of the Association for the Study of Higher Education, San Antonio, TX.

National Association of State Scholarship and Grant Programs (various years). *NASSGP/NASSGAP annual survey report.* Deerfield, IL; Harrisburg, PA; and Albany, NY: Illinois State Scholarship Commission; Pennsylvania Higher Education Assistance Agency; and New York State Higher Education Services Corporation.

National Association of State Student Grant and Aid Programs. (2003). *33rd annual survey report on state-sponsored student financial aid 2001-2002 academic year.* Albany: New York State Higher Education Services Corporation.

Potter, W. (2003, August 8). State lawmakers again cut higher-education spending. *The Chronicle of Higher Education, XLVII*(48), A22-A23.

Promise Scholarship Program. (2002). Welcome to Promise (http://www.promisescholarships.org/). Charleston, WV: Author.

Selingo, J. (2001, January 19). Questioning the merit of merit scholarships. *The Chronicle of Higher Education, XLVII*(19), A20-A22.

South Carolina Commission on Higher Education (2002). LIFE Scholarship (http://www.che400.state.sc.us/web/Student/ LIFE/LIFE%20home.html). Columbia: Author.

United States Bureau of the Census (2002). Table FINC-03, presence of related children under 18 years old-all families, by total money income in 2000 (http://ferret.bls.census.gov/macro/ 032001/faminc/new03_000.htm). Washington, DC: Author.

University of Alaska (2002). UA Scholars Program (http://www.alaska.edu/scholars/). Fairbanks: Author.

CHAPTER 6

FINANCIAL ACCESS: THE IMPACT OF STATE FINANCE STRATEGIES[1]

Edward P. St. John, Choong-Geun Chung,
Glenda D. Musoba, and Ada B. Simmons

Expanding college access using cost efficient means has become a major policy issue in most states. Attaining at least some postsecondary education—a degree from a two-year or four-year college—is increasingly necessary for employment (Pascarella & Terenzini 1991; Paulsen, 2001a, 2001b). While college funding was considered central to expanding access during most of the twentieth century, for the past two decades the debates about policies for expanding access have focused on implementing education reform and improving academic preparation of college students (King, 1999; National Center for Education Statistics [NCES], 1997a). As more high school students take the steps to prepare for college, it will be necessary for states to make efficient use of tax dollars in efforts to expand postsecondary opportunities for low-income students. Whether or not state education reforms are successful, there must be ample financial opportunity for qualified students to attend college.

The Advisory Committee on Student Financial Assistance (2002) estimated that about four million college-qualified students from low- and middle-income families would be denied access to four-year colleges in the first decade of the twenty-first century because the remaining costs of college, after loans and grants, would be higher than students could afford. However, there is great variability in access to two-year and four-year colleges across the states. Some states have extensive two-year college systems that provide an initial gateway to college. Other states provide ample grant aid to ensure that qualified students have access. Yet many do not provide adequate access at this time.

This chapter examines the impact of state financing strategies on college access in the 1990s and proposes a cost efficient approach for expanding access over the next decade. Because the debates about college access consider both academic preparation and financial access, the analyses consider the roles of both financial and academic factors. First, we describe the logical model and statistical methods used to develop a set of state financial indicators for the 1990s and to assess the impact of state financial strategies on college access and the study methods. Then we present analyses of the impact of state financial strategies on high school graduation rates and college enrollment rates during the 1990s using state financial indicators.

A Balanced Approach

Given the aim of assessing the impact of state financial strategies on college access, this study used a conceptual model that considers the issues raised by both economic studies of college access and recent policy studies of the academic correlates of four-year college enrollment.[2] This model is based on an understanding of social theory, research on educational attainment,[3] economic theory, and research on price response and public finance (St. John, 2003; St. John & Paulsen, 2001).

The conceptual model (Figure 1) recognizes that there is an educational attainment pipeline in states that can be influenced by the public finance strategies used in the state. The educational attainment pipeline is defined as:

 • *Demographic Context*: The ethnic composition of the state's population and the extent of wealth, poverty, and education.[4] The demographic context represents the state-level equivalent of variables for family income and parents' education, which are frequently used in studies of college access that use individual-level data.
 • *Academic Preparation*: While in studies of enrollment in four-year colleges it may be desirable to consider the specific courses that students take in high school, in most

states students are qualified for enrollment in a two-year college if they receive a high school diploma. Therefore, in the current study, which aims to examine access to two-year and four-year colleges, high school graduation rates represent the appropriate measure of academic preparation.

• *Postsecondary Attainment:* There are two types of indicators of the impact of public finance on college attainment:

1. Enrollment rates for high school graduates (and possibly enrollment in different sectors of state higher education systems); and
2. College graduation rates (or other measures of completion, such as the ratios of first time enrollment to degrees), which are not considered here because the data are not available.

The systems of public finance are the primary means that states can use to promote educational attainment, especially college attainment among state populations. The system of public finance in states links to the educational attainment pipeline in several ways:

• *Tax Rates:* Historically it was assumed that there were higher tax rates in states with wealthier populations, but many states either reduced some taxes or resisted tax increases in the 1980s and 1990s. Therefore, a state's tax rate, controlling for the wealth of the population, can influence both academic preparation and college attainment. The tax rate measure used here was total taxes collected by a state divided by personal income (from the U.S. Census Bureau).

• *School Funding:* The level of state funding for public K-12 education can be influenced by the wealth and tax rates in a state.[5] The level of school funding could influence the high school graduation rate in a state and has a direct effect on the availability of certain high school courses.

• *Expected Tuition and Grants:* Student expectations about tuition and grants can influence their desire to prepare for college (St. John, 2002). Therefore, there is reason to expect that average public tuition charges and

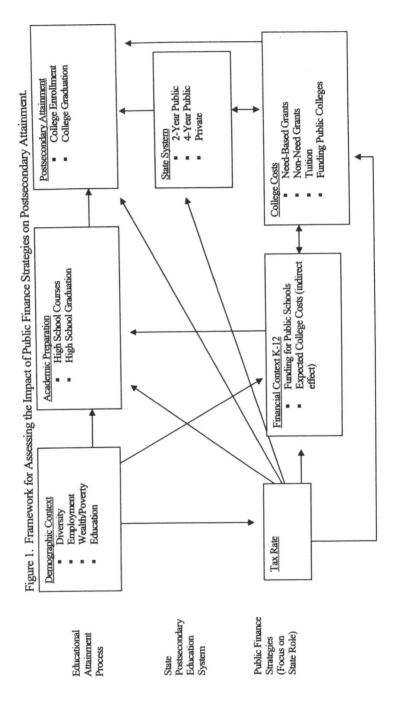

Figure 1. Framework for Assessing the Impact of Public Finance Strategies on Postsecondary Attainment.

average state grants two years prior to graduation can influence the high school graduation rate in a state.

• *Actual College Costs*: States finance college access and persistence through student grants (need-based and non-need) and tuition subsidies to public colleges. At a given level of educational expenditures by public colleges, state subsidies to public colleges reduce tuition charges to college students.

In addition to public finance strategies, the composition of the state postsecondary education system has an influence on college access. Extensive two-year college systems or a large number of independent colleges can expand access or provide different forms of access for different groups. In analyses of the impact of public finance strategies on access, it is appropriate to control for the structure of state systems of higher education.[6] In addition, some students who enroll in college attend colleges out of state, but out-of-state enrollment is not directly influenced by state finance strategies unless states provide grant subsidies to students who enroll out of state.[7]

Using this conceptual model, we examined the impact of demographic indicators and state financial strategies on academic preparation as measured by high school graduation rates[8] and college enrollment rates. The study team developed a statistical model, testing different measures. The information used in the study was developed as part of a state fiscal and financial aid indicators project being developed currently for Lumina Foundation for Education.

Research Approach

As a part of this study the project team developed a set of financial indicators that were used in the analysis of the impact of state financial strategies. Below we describe the indicators database, model specifications, statistical methods, and study limitations.

State Financial and Demographic Indicators
To test this model, the study team developed a set of financial and demographic indicators for each of the 50 states for the 1992, 1994, 1996, 1998, and 2000 fiscal years. All dollar amounts were adjusted to 2000 dollars. The analyses of high school graduation rates used financial indicators for two years

prior to graduation, to reflect the financial conditions that prevailed when students in a cohort were enrolled in high school and making future plans.

Annual reports by NCES in the Integrated Postsecondary Education Data System (IPEDS), as well as supplemental analyses provided by Tom Mortenson at Postsecondary Education Opportunity, provided educational attainment data. The indicators were:

- *High school graduation rate*, used as an outcome measure (calculated from NCES high school graduation data and the enrollment when the cohorts were in 9th grade).
- *College enrollment rate*, used as an outcome measure (fall enrollment reports were used to calculate the percentage of high school graduates enrolled in higher education in the following fall[9]).
- *Size of the 9th grade cohort*, used as an independent variable to control for population size (from NCES's Common Core of Data).

IPEDS was the primary data source for the financial indicators. Analysis of IPEDS represented a major part of the work required to complete this project, given the complexity of this information system.[10] IPEDS was used for information on:

- *College finances* (College tuition weighted per FTE).[11]
- *State system and college enrollment* (Fall enrollment data were used to develop weights[12] for financial indicators and to calculate the percentage of FTE students enrolled in the various sectors of higher education, public four-year, public two-year, and private colleges in the state. These analyses used total FTE rather than college freshmen enrollment because this provided a better indicator of capacity).

The other indicators related to public finance included:

- *Tax rate* (state tax collection in a given year divided by personal income, an indicator from U.S. Census Bureau, State Government Tax Collections).
- *Need-based grants adjusted per FTE* (Total need-based grants were derived from NASSGAP, Annual Survey Reports and divided by undergraduate FTE in the state).

- *Non-need grants adjusted per FTE* (The sum of total merit and other grants, calculated from NASSGAP, Annual Survey Reports, divided by undergraduate FTE).
- *K-12 expenditures per FTE* (NCES, National Public Education Financial Survey).

In addition, this study used the following state indicators, developed from other data sources:[13]

- *Percent poverty in the population*[14] (U.S. Census Bureau, Current Population Survey).
- *Percent African American* (U.S. Census Bureau, Population Estimates).
- *Percent Hispanic* (U.S. Census Bureau, Population Estimates).
- *Percent other minority* (calculated by adding the percentages of Native Americans and Asians and dividing by the state population, U.S. Census Bureau, Population Estimates).
- *Percent of the population with bachelor's degrees or higher*[15] (U.S. Census Bureau, Current Population Survey).

Using this method, a set of financial indicators was developed for each state which was used in the analyses of academic preparation and college graduation.

Model Specifications

When assessing the impact of state finance policies on high school graduation rates and college enrollment rates, it is appropriate to use linear models because the outcomes are continuous variables. This chapter presents the results of two fixed-effect regression analyses of the impact of public finance policies on access using the state indicators data.[16] Variables used in the regression predicting high school graduation rates are shown in Table 1.

Variables used in the analysis of the impact of public finance strategies on college enrollment of high school graduates are presented in Table 2. This approach provides a method of assessing the impact of financial aid—need-based and non-need— on enrollment rates in states, controlling for the effects of academic preparation.[17] Thus, this approach overcomes the most serious limitations of prior efforts to relate variations in public finance strategies to enrollment rates.

Table 1: Independent Variables Used in Analysis of High School Graduation Rates.

Demographic Context
Percent of the state population below the poverty level
Percent of African Americans in the population
Percent of Hispanics in the population
Percent of other minorities in the population
Size of the 9th grade cohort four years prior
Percent of the population with a Bachelor's degree or higher

Financial Controls
Tax rate
K-12 expenditures (two years before graduation)

Higher Education Finance Strategies
Need-based grants per FTE (two years before high school graduation)
Non-need grants per FTE (two years before high school graduation)
Tuition charges weighted per FTE (two years before high school graduation)

Table 2: Independent Variables Used in Analysis of College Enrollment Rates by High School Graduates.

o **Demographic Context** (See independent variables used in Table 1)
o **Financial Controls** (Tax rate)
o **Higher Education Finance Strategies**
1. Need-based grants per FTE (for first year of college eligibility)
2. Non-need grants per FTE (for first year of college eligibility)
3. Tuition charges weighted per FTE (first year of college eligibility)

Statistical Methods

Regression analysis is appropriate for the analysis of the impact of financial policies on graduation and enrollment rates because both outcomes are continuous variables. Further, most of the indictors used in the regression analyses were continuous variables.

The study team considered using ordinary least squares regression, but after careful review decided to use fixed-effects regression. The fixed effects regression method was appropriate because it provided a method of controlling for state effects using coding (or effects) variables. In addition to the financial and demographic forces, academic policies in states can influence access (see Chapter 7). Using the fixed-effects method, a variable is calculated for unspecified characteristics, including state education policies. Thus, in this model we are able to control for the effects of other policies in states without actually specifying those variables.

The two regression tables provide both standardized and unstandardized coefficients, levels of significance (.1, .05, and .01). The lowest of these levels (.1) indicates only a modest association and we are cautious about reaching any conclusions about these associations. In addition, R^2 and P-values are presented as indicators of the quality of the models.

Limitations

First, like all regression analyses, these analyses should not be interpreted as causal. Rather, the use of sound logic to select variables provides a basis for assuming that the variables included in the model have an influence on the outcomes. The logic framework, reviewed above, was used to guide the variable selection process. The analyses reported here represent the initial test of the new logical approach to the study of college access.

Second, the analyses cannot be generalized beyond the period studied. While similar financial conditions have persisted into the early 2000s, there have been major changes in the economies across the states that could limit the implications of these analyses. Thus, this study provides an evaluation of the impact of finance strategies used in the 1990s.

The Impact of State Public Finance Strategies

While the first aim of this study—to measure the effects of state public finance strategies on access—may seem straightforward, it is a complex process that is further complicated by methodological considerations. To illuminate the role of public finance in promoting access, this chapter examines both academic preparation (high school graduation rates), as an indicator of the indirect effects of financial aid, and college enrollment (by high school graduates), as an indicator of the direct effects of financial strategies.

High School Graduation Rates

Logically, state funding for financial aid had an indirect effect on college enrollment rates because it influences the will of low-income students to finish high school (Advisory Committee on Student Financial Assistance, 2002; St. John, 2003). High school graduation rates were influenced by the demographic context of the state and the strategies used to finance higher education, controlling for public finance of schools (Table 3). Three of the demographic variables were significant in the fixed-effects regression analysis. The percentage of Hispanics in a state's population was positively associated with high school graduation. The percentage of the population that are other minorities and the percentage that had a bachelor's degree or higher were negatively associated with high school graduation rates.

The reasons why education level was negatively associated with high school graduation rates are complex and merit further study. The fixed-effects analysis statistically controls for the state context. First, we can only speculate about the explanations of the finding on education levels of the population. If states import highly educated citizens, they may have artificially depressed high school graduation rates in these statistical models because the population with children is less well-educated (on average) than new citizens attracted to these states. Alternatively, an educated citizenry could keep educational standards high, which may dissuade low-achieving students. Second, high school graduation rates actually declined in the 1990s, which adds to the complexity of interpreting this finding. The decline in graduation rates is partially attributable to the impact of state education reforms. The impact of school reforms is "controlled for" by the state variables implicit in fixed-effects models. Therefore, the effects of some reforms could confound these analyses.

Table 3: Fixed-Effect Regression: The Influence of Population Characteristics and State Finance Strategies on Public High School Graduation Rate in the 1990s.

	Regression Coeff.		Sig.
	Unstand	Standard	
% Poverty	0.063	0.025	
% African American	0.774	0.803	
% Hispanic	1.222	1.103	*
% Other Minorities	-5.356	-5.366	***
Enrollment when the Cohort was 9th Grade	0.000	0.262	
% of Population with Bachelor's Degree or Higher	-0.310	-0.151	**
Tax Rate (=State Tax Collection / Personal Income)	0.100	0.015	
Per Student K-12 Expenditures ($/1,000) 2 Years Prior	-0.003	-0.027	
Per FTE Need-Based Grant Amount ($/1,000) 2 Years Prior	0.031	0.094	
Per FTE Non-Need Grant Amount ($/1,000) 2 Years Prior	-0.061	-0.097	**
Undergraduate In-State Tuition and Fees for Public System ($/1,000) 2 Years Prior	-0.321	-0.371	***
Adjusted R square	0.933		
N	200		
P-value for F test that all $u_i=0$ [1]			0.000

Note: *** $p<0.01$, ** $p<0.05$, * $p<0.1$

1. The null hypothesis of the F test is that the state-specific, fixed-effect terms are all zeroes. The fixed-effect model can be judged to be significantly different from the OLS model when we reject the null hypothesis.

This analysis of the influence of demographic variables raises questions about the influence of a state's demographic composition on high school graduates. The fixed-effects approach controls for specific state contexts in a set of uncoded variables for the state. When this approach is used, the education level of the population has a substantially different effect on high school graduation rates than we would expect from research on academic preparation. This suggests that further research is needed on the effects of school reform policies on high school graduation rates. Tuition charges and state grants, both measured two years prior to graduation, also had an influence on high school graduation rates. Both tuition charges and non-need grants were negatively associated with high school graduation rates. Need-based grants were not significant, but had a positive association with high school graduation rates. Higher need-based grants could have a slight positive association with high school graduation rates, while higher merit-based grants would negatively influence graduation rates. This statistical association may be because students with low grades believe they cannot afford to attend college in their states if they do not maintain the grade point requirements necessary to attain merit-based grants.

College Enrollment Rates
State finance strategies had a substantial and direct effect on college enrollment by high school graduates, controlling for demographic contexts and the structure of higher education in the states. The fixed-effect regression analysis revealed that demographic context, state system capacity, and student grants have an influence on enrollment (Table 4).

While the poverty level in a state was not statistically associated with high school graduation rates (Table 3), it was significant and negatively associated with college enrollment rates (Table 4). Low-income families are clearly more disadvantaged with respect to college enrollment than to high school graduation. The percentage of the population with college degrees was also positively associated with college enrollment rates, further indicating that demographic variables related to socioeconomic status (SES) have a substantial and direct influence on college enrollment by students who prepared academically for college by graduating from high school.

Table 4: Fixed-Effect Regression: The Influence of Population Characteristics and State Finance Strategies on College Enrollment Rate in the 1990s.

	Regression Coeff.		Sig.
	Unstand	Standard	
% Poverty	-0.462	-0.238	***
% African American	-1.810	-2.326	
% Hispanic	-1.174	-1.316	*
% Other Minorities	2.388	3.001	
Enrollment when the Cohort was 9th Grade	-0.000	-0.694	*
% of Population with Bachelor's Degree or Higher	0.299	0.182	*
% Public 2 Year Institution FTE	0.211	0.328	*
% Private Institution FTE	0.643	1.089	***
Tax Rate (=State Tax Collection / Personal Income)	-0.071	-0.015	
Per FTE Need-Based Grant Amount ($/1,000)	0.115	0.426	***
Per FTE Non-Need Grant Amount ($/1,000)	0.089	0.204	***
Undergrad In-State Tuition and Fees for Public System ($/1,000)	0.100	0.146	
Adjusted R square	0.789		
N	244		
P-value for F test that all u_i=0	0.000		

Note: *** $p<0.01$, ** $p<0.05$, * $p<0.1$

The capacity of state higher education systems also expands postsecondary opportunity. The percentages of students enrolled both in community colleges and private colleges were positively associated with enrollment rates in the states. Tax capacity was not associated with college enrollment.

Both need-based grants and non-need grants were significant and positively associated with enrollment rates, although the direct effects of need-based aid were much more substantial (twice the influence). The more modest effects of non-need grants were related to state contexts. In contrast, tuition charges were not significantly associated with enrollment. Thus, the most efficient way for states to expand access is to increase funding for need-based grants, especially when tuition increases.

The Impact of Public Finance Strategies

These analyses provide substantial new insights into the impact of public finance policies on access. Student financial assistance has both direct and indirect effects on access. If students feel they cannot afford to attend college, either because of high tuition charges or the restrictions on state grants, they are less likely to graduate from high school. In contrast, need-based grants were positively related to academic preparation (although not significantly related in the fixed-effects regression) and positively and significantly associated with college enrollment by high school graduates.

Conclusions and Implications

While there has been substantial disagreement in the policy literature about underlying causes of the current access challenge, there is general agreement that college access should be expanded, especially for college-prepared, low-income students. Based on a review of this literature, this study has used a balanced logical model to assess the effects of state finance strategies on high school graduation rates and college enrollment rates. The analyses reveal that finances have a modest indirect effect on academic preparation, as indicated by analyses of high school graduation rates, as well as a substantial direct influence on college enrollment.

There is a substantial body of research indicating state grants influence persistence (St. John, 2003), even though it was not possible to examine persistence in this study. State-level studies have found that funding for state need-based grants helped equalize the opportunity for persistence in Washington state (St. John, 1999) and Indiana (Hu & St. John, 2001; St. John, Hu, & Weber, 2000, 2001). Further, Indiana's Twenty-first Century Scholars Program has been shown to influence academic preparation, college enrollment, and college persistence for low-income high school students (St. John, Musoba, Simmons, & Chung, 2002; St. John, Musoba, Simmons, Schmit, Chung, & Peng, 2002). Thus, state grants improve retention as well as access.

During the 1990s, states allowed public tuition charges to rise when they lacked tax revenues to provide continuity in funding for state colleges and universities. However, funding of state grants did not increase at a rate that would have been needed to ensure financial access for low-income students. Had states coordinated increases in state grants with increases in tuition, substantially more college-qualified students would have had the opportunity to enroll in college.

Allowing tuition to rise and investing sufficiently in student grants represents a more efficient use of tax dollars than providing general subsidies to institutions benefiting all students enrolled in public colleges. When states shift away from investing in institutions and allow tuition to rise, a pattern evident over the past two decades, they have a moral obligation to provide sufficient grant aid for qualified low- and middle-income students. In the 1990s, most states fell short of meeting the minimum equity standard of funding for need-based grants at a level equaling one-quarter of public sector tuition changes.

Notes

1.   Lumina Foundation for Education funded this study and released an earlier version of this analysis. Derek V. Price (Director of Higher Education Research), Jerry S. Davis (Vice President for Research), and Robert C. Dickeson (Senior Vice President for Higher Education Policy) of Lumina Foundation provided reviews and guidance for this study. The advisory panel for this project included: Derek V. Price, Jerry S. Davis, Jill Wohlford, and Deborah Bonnet (Lumina Foundation for Education), Cheryl Blanco (Western Interstate Commission for Higher Education), Brian Fitzgerald (Advisory Committee on Student Financial Assistance), Susan Kleeman (Illinois Student Assistance Commission), Donald Heller (Center for the Study of Higher Education at Pennsylvania State University), Paul Lingenfelter (State Higher Education Executive Officers), Tom Mortenson (Pell Center for the Study of Opportunity in Higher Education), Laura Perna (University of Maryland), Kenneth Redd (National Association of Student Financial Aid Administrators), Scott Thomas (Institute for Higher Education-University of Georgia), and Nick Vesper (State Student Assistance Commission of Indiana). The opinions expressed in this chapter are those of the authors and do not necessarily reflect policies or positions of

Lumina Foundation for Education or members of the project advisory panel. In addition, the authors thank Ontario Wooden and Jesse Mendez for their support on this study, especially the companion report on state financial indicators.

2.   The analyses of college enrollment by NCES have used an "academic pipeline" model (NCES, 1997a, 1997b, 2000, 2001a, 2001b) that is loosely based on the logic of social theory of educational attainment.   However, these reports have generally failed to make this logic explicit and to recognize that finances also influence enrollment rates.   Instead these studies have tended to focus on specific high school courses that correlate with eventual college enrollment without considering the role of academic courses within a theory of attainment that would identify appropriate units for measuring academic preparation and educational attainment.   It is appropriate to refer to this type of analysis as seeking correlates of enrollment that are consistent with beliefs or ideologies, rather than as a theory-based approach to evaluation.

3.   The measurement of the impact of social variables (i.e., parents' education and income) on educational attainment is rooted in sociological theory and research (Alexander & Eckland, 1974, 1977, 1978; Blau & Duncan, 1967) and recent studies that examine social capital formation (Ellwood & Kane, 2000; Hearn, 2001; Steelman & Powell, 1993).

4.   This study tested the use of both poverty rates and income per capita.   However, the two variables were highly correlated, therefore poverty rate was used as a predictor because it related more directly to the financial access issues that were of concern in this report.   In addition, since tax rates were used in the analyses, we had an additional statistical control for the influence of wealth. In response to inquiries from reviewers of an earlier version of this analysis, the study team also tested the use of unemployment rates as a predictor variable.   However, as expected, unemployment was very highly correlated with poverty rate; therefore, it was not included in the final model.

5.   This study controls for the influence of school funding, but not school reform policies. High school graduation rates dropped during the 1990s, a period during which more stringent requirements were implemented.   Therefore, to fully assess the impact of school funding on graduation rates, it was also necessary to examine the impact of school reform policies (see Chapter 7).

6. In earlier analyses, the research team had developed separate analyses of enrollment rates in public two-year colleges, public four-year colleges, private colleges, and colleges in other states. The project advisory committee suggested modifying the base access model to consider the role of system complexity, as an alternative to presenting a larger number of statistical models. In particular, Laura Perna was helpful in conceptualizing the role of system capacity in the access models presented in the paper.

7. The early analyses included an analysis of the impact of state financial strategies on the percentage of high school graduates who enroll out of state. These analyses will be published separately, along with the analyses of the impact of state financial strategies on the distribution of high school graduates within state systems.

8. In analyses of the impact of state financial strategies on academic preparation, high school graduation rate is a more appropriate indicator than high school courses. First, high school graduation is a better indicator of preparation for two-year and four-year colleges than are specific courses related to a college preparatory curriculum, which may be a better indicator of preparation for four-year enrollment. Further, state policies that require more students to take advanced courses in high school could have the unintended effect of reducing high school graduation rates. Therefore it is more appropriate to assess the effects of school reform policies on high school graduation rates, as an indicator of the efficacy of state reforms, than to use high school curricula to constrain analyses of college enrollment. Even if better indicators of high school curricula had been available, it would not have been inappropriate to use such indicators in this study.

9. The study team used IPEDS, along with data reported annually by Tom Mortenson in the Postsecondary Education Opportunity newsletter and available from http://postsecondary.org. Using NCES data, Mortenson calculated college continuation rates by state, based on the number of high school graduates from the Current Population Survey of the Census Bureau and college freshmen from the IPEDS Fall Enrollment.

10. It was frequently necessary to sum information for campuses and states across different data files in order to develop appropriate indicators.

11. Education revenues and expenditures as well as state appropriations were considered in preliminary analyses but not included in the final model.

12. Tuition charges in public colleges were weighted for each state to reflect the actual pattern of enrollment in the state. The number of undergraduates enrolling in each public college was multiplied by the undergraduate in-state tuition charge for the college; then these numbers were summed and divided by the total number of undergraduates enrolling in the state. This weighted tuition charge reflects the composition of enrollment in the state.

13. These indicators were generally available as state averages. We generated these indicators by abstracting information from published sources, which did not require the extensive reanalysis necessary to work with the cumbersome IPEDS databases.

14. We also examined other possible indicators related to state economic conditions, including unemployment rates and income per capita.

15. This variable provides a logical control for the influence of parents' education. There is a high correlation between the percentage of high school students in a state whose parents attended college and the percentage of the population with a four-year degree or higher. We also tested the inclusion of a variable for the percent of the population with at least a high school diploma and/or some college. Including this variable had no discernable effect on the results, so it was left out of the final model.

16. Fixed-effects regression provides the appropriate method of analysis given the fact that multiple years (or a time series) are included in the data set. The fixed-effects method provides a means of controlling for the state context. Don Heller, a member of the Advisory Committee, consulted with the research team on the selection of a regression method.

17. The readers are reminded that since this analysis considers the population that has graduated from high school, it controls for the effects of academic preparation. Further, high school graduation is a more appropriate measure of preparation for enrollment in state systems (inclusive of community colleges).

References

Advisory Committee on Student Financial Assistance. (2002). *Empty promises: The myth of college access in America.* Washington, DC: Author.

Alexander, K. L., & Eckland, B. K. (1974). Sex differences in the educational attainment process. *American Sociological Review, 39*(5), 668-682.

Alexander, K. L., & Eckland, B. K. (1977). High school context and college selectivity: Institutional constraints in educational stratification. *Social Forces, 56*(1), 166-188.

Alexander, K. L., & Eckland, B. K. (1978). Basic attainment processes: A replication and extension, 1999. *Sociology of Education, 48,* 457-495.

Blau, P., & Duncan, O. D. (1967). *The American occupational structure.* New York: Wiley.

Ellwood, D., & Kane, T. J. (2000). Who is getting a college education: Family background and the growing gaps in enrollment. In S. Danziger & J. Waldfogel (Eds.), *Securing the future: Investing in children from birth to college.* (pp. 283-324) New York: Russell Sage Foundation.

Hearn, J. C. (2001). Access to postsecondary education: Financing equity in an evolving context. In M. B. Paulsen & J. B. Smart (Eds.), *The finance of higher education: Theory, research, policy & practice* (pp. 419-439). New York: Agathon Press.

Hu, S., & St. John, E. P. (2001). Student persistence in a public higher education system: Understanding racial/ethnic difference. *Journal of Higher Education, 72*(3), 265-286.

King, J. E. (Ed.). (1999). *Financing a college education: How it works, how it is changing.* Phoenix, AZ: Orynx Press.

National Center for Education Statistics. (1997a). *Access to higher postsecondary education for the 1992 high school graduates,* NCES 98-105. By Lutz Berkner & Lisa Chavez. Project Officer: C. Dennis Carroll. Washington, DC: Author.

National Center for Education Statistics. (1997b). *Confronting the odds: Students at risk and the pipeline to higher education.* NCES 98-094. By Laura J. Horn. Project Officer: C. Dennis Carroll. Washington, DC: Author.

National Center for Education Statistics. (2000). *Mapping the road to college: First-generation students' math track, planning strategies, and context of support.* NCES 2000-153. By Laura Horn & Anne-Marie Nunez. Project Officer: Larry Bobbitt. Washington, DC: Author.

National Center for Education Statistics. (2001a). *Bridging the gap: Academic preparation and postsecondary success of first-generation students.* NCES 2001-153. By Edward C. Warburton

128   *Financial Access: The Impact of State Finance Strategies*

& Rosio Bugarin. Project Officer: C. Dennis Carroll. Washington, DC: Author.

National Center for Education Statistics. (2001b). *Students whose parents did not go to college: Postsecondary access, persistence, and attainment.* By Susan Choy. Washington, DC: Author.

Pascarella, E. T., & Terenzini, P. T. (1991). *How college affects students.* San Francisco: Jossey-Bass.

Paulsen, M. B. (2001a). The economics of human capital and investment in higher education. In M. B. Paulsen & J. C. Smart (Eds.), *The finance of higher education: Theory, research, policy & practice* (pp. 55-94). New York: Agathon Press.

Paulsen, M. B. (2001b). The economics of the public sector: The nature of public policy in higher education finance. In M. B. Paulsen & J. C. Smart (Eds.), *The finance of higher education: Theory, research, policy & practice* (pp. 95-132). New York: Agathon Press.

St. John, E. P. (1999). Evaluating state grant programs: A case study of Washington's grant program. *Research in Higher Education, 40*(2), 149-170.

St. John, E. P. (2002). *The access challenge: Rethinking the causes of the new inequality.* Policy Issue Report # 2002-01. Bloomington, IN: Indiana Education Policy Center.

St. John, E. P. (2003). *Refinancing the college dream: Access, equal opportunity, and justice for taxpayers.* Baltimore: Johns Hopkins University Press.

St. John, E. P., Hu, S., & Weber, J. (2000). Keeping public colleges affordable: A study of persistence in Indiana's public colleges and universities. *Journal of Student Financial Aid, 30*(1), 21-32.

St. John, E. P., Hu, S., & Weber, J. (2001). State policy and the affordability of public higher education: The influence of state grants on persistence in Indiana. *Research in Higher Education, 42*(4), 401-428.

St. John, E. P., Musoba, G. D., Simmons, A. B., & Chung, C. G. (2002). *Meeting the access challenge: Indiana's Twenty-first Century Scholars Program.* New Agenda Series, vol. 4, no. 4. Indianapolis: Lumina Foundation for Education.

St. John, E. P., Musoba, G. D., Simmons, A. B., Schmit, J., Chung, C. G., & Peng, C-Y. J. (November, 2002). *Meeting the access challenge: An examination of Indiana's Twenty-first*

Century Scholars Program. Prepared for the Association for the Study of Higher Education Annual Meeting, Sacramento, CA.

St. John, E. P., & Noell, J. (1989). The impact of financial aid on access: An analysis of progress with special consideration of minority access. *Research in Higher Education, 30*(6), 563-582.

St. John, E. P., & Paulsen, M. B. (2001). The finance of higher education: Implications for theory, research, policy, and practice. In M. B. Paulsen & J. C. Smart (Eds.), *The finance of higher education: Theory, research, policy & practice* (pp. 11-38). New York: Agathon.

Steelman, L. C., & Powell, B. (1993). Doing the right thing: Race and parental locus of responsibility for funding college. *Sociology of Education, 66*(4), 223-244.

CHAPTER 7

ACADEMIC ACCESS: THE IMPACT OF STATE EDUCATION POLICIES

Edward P. St. John, Glenda D. Musoba,
and Choong-Geun Chung

Introduction

Increasingly, education reforms in the United States are rationalized as means of improving access to higher education (Adelman, 2002). School reforms such as increased math requirements for high school graduation, raising educational standards, aligning curriculum and standards, using standardized tests as high school graduation requirements, and using merit-based grant aid are rationalized based on the assumption that academic barriers impede access to higher education. This logic is supported by the federal *No Child Left Behind Act* (NCLB) and is reflected in policy changes over the past two decades.

While the academic preparation rationale was based on analyses of the relationship between high school courses and college enrollment (e.g., NCES, 1997a; Pelavin & Kane, 1988), the policies themselves have seldom been systematically evaluated. Specifically, the linkages between state education reforms and college enrollment have not been examined. This chapter examines the evolution of the academic preparation rationale, the research approach used to examine the impact of state reforms, and the analysis of the impact of state education policies using a state-level database, then considers the implications of these analyses for K-12 and higher education.

131

The Academic Preparation Rationale

The notion that reform agendas are "rationales" provides a means for discerning the specific elements of claims behind reforms and for evaluating these reforms (St. John, in press). The steps involved in this type of evaluation involve reviewing the new logic used in research related to the rationale, discerning policies that are based on this logic, and examining the impact of the new policies. To understand the academic preparation rationale, it is necessary first to consider the research on college access and school reform that guided state policy on high school reform, then to identify the specific policies that relate to this rationale.

Research on Academic Access

In the 1980s the Office of Education Research and Improvement (OERI) in the U.S. Department of Education (USED) undertook initiatives to shift the focus of educational policy from being concerned about equal educational opportunity and equity in funding, to being concerned about test scores. Chester Finn, Jr., the Assistant Secretary for OERI, argued this shift refocused policy on the outcome of education, rather than input and process (Finn, 1990). The logic of research funded by USED also shifted to the linkages between academic preparation and educational outcomes.

These changes in education philosophy directly influenced higher education policy research. In response to criticisms of the growing gap in enrollment rates for African Americans compared to Whites by representatives (e.g., Wilson, 1986) in the American Council on Education (ACE) and other national lobbying organizations, the Reagan administration requested a study of the opportunity gap. At the time, there was concern that decreases in funding for the Pell grant program could be contributing to the decline in enrollment by low-income students (Kramer, 1982; St. John & Byce, 1982), as well as speculation that the Pell grants had not made a difference in access (Hansen, 1983).

The contractors for the research on the enrollment gap overlooked the issue of financial aid by focusing on the linkage between high school courses and college enrollment. These studies obfuscated the issue when they noted that enrollment of African Americans was rising faster than that of Whites (Chaikind, 1987; Pelavin & Kane, 1988) and noted that the intent of federal student aid was to improve access for low-income students (Pelavin & Kane, 1988, 1990). However, these reports failed to consider that enrollment growth (numbers of students) was an artifact of differentials in population growth rates, and that enrollment rates (percentages of students going to college) provided better indicators of the gap. They also failed to note, when summarizing the intent of aid programs, that federal grant aid had declined. In other words, they shifted the logic of the debate from an explicit concern about financial access, to an explicit focus on academic preparation as a means of attaining access.

The most cited finding from these studies was that taking algebra in middle school was associated with college enrollment (Pelavin & Kane, 1990). Subsequent analyses used this logic to analyze the National Educational Longitudinal Study (NELS:88), a large scale panel survey following students in the high school class of 1992 from high school through college. NELS has been used to examine the math courses high school students take (Adelman, 1999) and to develop an index of high school courses indicating the extent of college qualification (NCES, 1997a).

NCES has made substantial use of the database to study the role of academic preparation in college enrollment. The NCES (1997b) model, the pipeline to college, defines the following steps:

- Step 1: Aspirations
- Step 2: Academic Preparation
- Step 3: Entrance Exams
- Step 4: College Application
- Step 5: Enrollment

The analyses using this model (NCES, 1997a; 1997b; 2000) systematically overlooked the idea that finances influence enrollment behavior, even when they reported statistics on financial aid (e.g., NCES, 1997a). The following conclusion illustrates the interpretative position typically taken in these federal reports:

Although there are differences by income and race-ethnicity in the four-year college enrollment rates of college-qualified high school graduates, the difference between college-qualified low-income and middle-income students, as well as difference among college-qualified black, Hispanic, Asian, and white students, are eliminated among those students who have taken the college entrance examinations and completed an application for admission, the two steps necessary to attend a four-year college. (NCES, 1997a, p. iii)

This statement clearly argues that by taking college entrance tests and applying in advance to four-year colleges,[1] minority students could gain access to four-year colleges. Ironically, this report presented information related to the role of finances, controlling for academic preparation, but in its conclusions failed to even consider the possibility that financial aid influenced college enrollment. Like most of NCES' other studies (NCES, 1996, 1997b) that have analyzed NELS, this report ignored the possibility that the decline in federal student aid after 1980 could have influenced the opportunity gap. The extreme nature of these claims about academic access necessitates a rethinking of the logical models used in federal studies of financial access.

Most recently, a summary report of the NCES analyses using this new academic access logic was published as part of the *Condition of Education* (NCES, 2002). A refined version of this report was published by ACE (Choy, 2002). The revised report reached the following conclusions about access:

- A young person's likelihood of attending a four-year college increases with the level of his or her parents' education. This is true even for the most highly-qualified high school seniors.
- Taking challenging mathematics courses can mitigate the effects of parents' education on college enrollment. The association between taking a rigorous high school math curriculum and going to college is strong for all students, but especially for those whose parents did not go beyond high school.
- More at-risk students apply to college if their friends plan to go. College outreach programs, as well as parental and school support with the application process, also have proven worthwhile.
- The price of attending is still a significant obstacle for students from low- and middle-income families, but

financial aid is an equalizer, to some degree. Low-income students enroll at the same rate as middle-income students if they take the steps toward enrollment. (Choy, 2002, p. 5)

Other aspects of the educational policy environment remain relatively stable. Honors diploma policies had been implemented in 17 states by 1991 and remained relatively stable over the decade, while implementation of several other policies grew substantially. State policies for high school exit exams fluctuated from 17 states in 1991 to a high of 23 states in 1999, but dropped to 20 in 2000. The average state participation rate in the SAT also remained relatively flat over the decade.

Choy (2002) carried forward the pipeline concept, but situates it within the context of parents' education. She argues that taking advanced math courses can help students to overcome the limitations of family background, applying to college is related to the behavior of peers, and student aid is working. A closer review of Choy's paper and the ones summarized in these reports reveals that the logic rests on the correlation between math courses and both college application and enrollment (St. John, 2003). However, these reports do not consider any policy variables—student aid or state education policies.

The sad irony of this ACE report is that while earlier publications (Wilson, 1986) by ACE helped stimulate the initial inquiries into the issue of the new inequality in access, this lobbying organization later published reports carrying forward the new logic of academic preparation and access. The speculation of the early ACE reports appears to be correct; the enrollment gap that opened in the early 1980s appears to be largely the result of the decline in need-based grants (Advisory Committee on Student Financial Assistance, 2002; St. John, 2003). However, enrollment rates for African Americans and Whites did improve in the 1990s, so it is worthwhile to examine if the education policies that are aligned with the new logic had an influence on academic access.

Policy Development
States used research by NCES to rationalize their education policies, just as the federal government used these reports to rationalize federal education legislation, such as NCLB. The types of education policies that are aligned with the new academic preparation logic include:

- Instituting "honors" diplomas for high school programs with advanced math courses and other advanced courses,
- Implementing math standards that are compatible with the National Council of Teachers of Mathematics (NCTM) recommendations, a generally accepted approach,
- Encouraging high schools to offer advanced placement (AP) courses, especially in math,
- Requiring high school exit examinations for high school graduation,
- Requiring three or more math courses for high school graduation, as contrasted to the usual requirement of one or two courses,
- Encouraging students to take the SAT or ACT test.

Table 1. Trends in the Implementation of High School Reforms in the Fifty States.

Education Reform	1991	1993	1995	1997	1999	2001
States w/ Honors Diploma	17	17	17	17	18	17
States w/ NCTM	12	28	46	50	50	50
Avg % schools w/AP courses	44.31	47.78	49.92	51.25	53.95	55.11
States w/ Exit Exams	17	19	19	17	23	20
States w/ 3+ Math	11	10	16	18	21	25
States w/ 1-2 Math	34	34	28	27	25	20
States w/ Local Control	6	7	7	6	5	5
Adjusted K-12 instructional exp. 2 years prior/FTE Avg. $(1000)	2.96	3.29	3.36	3.44	3.54	3.65
SAT Part. Rate* Nat. Avg.	36.32	37.14	35.59	34.82	37.00	37.00
Number of states with full data	51	51	51	51	51	50

*Participation rate here is an average of the state average participation rates, therefore the averages are lower than the national averages reported by the College Board which takes into account the size of the state cohorts.

State policies on national requirements changed substantially during the decade of the 1990s (see Table 1), as did other policies related to preparatory curricula. While only 12 states had math standards that were consistent with NCTM recommendations, that number grew to 100 percent adoption in 1997. Math standards progressively rose from only 11 states requiring three or more years of study in 1991 to 25 states having that policy in 2001, yet a relatively stable minority of states maintained local control. The average percentage of schools offering Advanced Placement courses in a state also grew steadily—from 44 percent to 55 percent. The advocates of the academic preparation rationale argue that educational outcomes are not related to educational expenditures (Finn, 1990, 2001; Paige, 2003). Therefore, unlike prior periods when the academic rationale was used to argue for increased education funding, this was not the case in the 1990s. However, K-12 instructional expenditures progressively rose from an average of $2,960 per student in 1991 to $3,650 per student in 2001 even when adjusted for inflation.

Assessing the Effects of Education Reforms

A critical step has been left out of the logic used for the academic access rationale and related efforts to increase regulation and measurement in K-12 education. Arguments for the reform are largely based on correlation statistics generated from studies of high school course taking, enhanced by the new regulatory logic made explicit in NCLB. However, the reformers have failed to evaluate systematically whether these reforms led to improvements in educational outcomes. Three outcomes are logically related to these policies: test scores as a measure of achievement, high school graduation (and drop out) rates, and college enrollment rates for graduates. Trends in three related indicators are examined in Table 2. There is some evidence of improvement in two of these trends during the decade. SAT scores improved modestly and college enrollment rates rose, while the high school graduation rate declined. Are these changes in outcomes related to the new education reform policies?

Research Approach

To address this question, we developed a state-level database from information on the 50 states. The analyses consider the effect of population characteristics and state education policies on each of these policy outcomes. Below we describe the database, statistical methods, and data limitations.

Table 2. Trends in SAT scores, high school graduation rates, and college enrollment rates for high school graduates.

Year	Combined SAT Nat. Avg.	High School Grad Rate, Nat. Avg.	College Enrollment Rate, Nat. Avg.
1991	999	71.2%	*
1992	1001	71.2%	53.31%
1994	1003	70.0%	55.67%
1996	1013	67.9%	56.39%
1998	1017	67.8%	56.85%
2000	1019	67.1%	56.88%

*data not available

Sources: SAT score: College Board; Graduation Rate: Postsecondary Opportunity Web site, *Chance for College by Age 19 by State*; College Enrollment: Postsecondary Opportunity Web site.

State Database

A multiyear database (1991 through 2000) was compiled from a number of government and private sources. Variables were state-level policy and achievement data. For the outcome variables, recentered SAT scores were gathered from the annual national reports of the College Board, and high school graduation rates and college-going rates (enrollment the fall following high school graduation) were calculated by Tom Mortensen and are available on the *Postsecondary Opportunity Newsletter* Web site. State policies for honors or advanced diplomas were collected in a survey by the Council of Chief State School Officers (CCSSO) and published in the *Digest of Education Statistics*. This was coded as a dichotomous variable for each year with a value of one if the state had a policy and a value of zero if the state did not. Assessments of whether the state's mathematic content standards were in compliance with NCTM recommendations were also collected in the same survey by the CCSSO. The year of first compliance data was converted to a dichotomous variable. The percent of schools in each state participating in the AP program and offering AP courses was drawn from the College Board web site. An alternative variable, the percent of students in the state taking an AP exam, was also available for some years, but preliminary testing showed that these two variables functioned in a similar manner in the regression (both significant and in the same direction in a test run) and correlated highly with one another. Because the percentage of schools rather than students is more under policy control, it was selected.

State exit exam policies are reported in the State Student Assessment Database from NCES. This was cross referenced with CCSSO survey data published in the *Digest of Education Statistics*. This was coded as a dichotomous variable, whether or not the state has an exam. Math graduation curriculum requirements were also compiled by the CCSSO and were reported in the *Condition of Education*. The number of credits in math required for graduation was collapsed into three groups: high (three or more), low (one to two), and states that allow local school boards to control graduation requirements. Data on the average K-12 school funding for each state was available from the NCES Web site. Only instructional expenditures were counted, and expenditures were divided by the enrollment or FTE to get a per student expenditure, and rescaled by dividing by 1000. The state average SAT participation rate is published each year in the annual national report from College Board and is available on their Web site.

If a data point for a state policy variable was missing for a particular year, the value from the prior year was carried forward. This was appropriate because most policies remain in place once implemented. When the particular policy was considered under development, in the year it was reported as under development we assumed it could not reasonably be expected to affect achievement; therefore, in dichotomous variables it was coded "no." State-level demographic data provided controls for those demographic variables known to be associated with achievement. For instance, the state educational attainment level, as measured by the percent of adults with a bachelor's degree or higher, also serves as a proxy for the average parent education level in the state. State-level education data was collected from the Current Population Survey conducted by the U.S. Census Bureau. Average state poverty levels, collected by the U.S. Census Bureau, were used as an approximation for the financial status of the citizenry in the state. The ethnic composition of the state, as collected through the Common Core of Data, represents the state demographic context.

Statistical Methods

These analyses used a fixed-effects ordinary least squares regression procedure. The fixed-effects procedure is most appropriate for time series or repeat measures data because it takes into account the association between the values within each state over time. Regression analyses used data from 1991 through 2000 and were conducted with STATA 8.0 software.

Study Limitations

Using a state-level database provides a logical approach for examining the relationship between policies and these state-level outcomes. Further, by controlling for demographic characteristics that can influence these outcomes, we provide a logical approach for assessing the relationship between high school policies and outcomes related to academic access. However, like any study, this approach has some limitations.

First, given the relatively small number of states and large number of policies, there were limits to the number of population variables we could use in this model. Given these constraints, we went through a number of steps to refine the model. We combined Current Population Surveys (CPS) statistical categories on ethnicity to come up with three distinct measures. We tested different measures of education level, including using both the percent of high school graduates and bachelors' graduates in the state populations, but concluded that the single measure was appropriate. We also tested other measures of wealth and income, but concluded that state poverty rate was the most appropriate predictor.

Second, the SAT is not the only college entrance examination. Not only were ACT scores not available for all of the years studied, but the SAT is widely used as an outcome indicator of education quality for K-12 education (College Board, 2001; LeFevre & Hederman, 2001). However, we took steps to consider the consequences of using SAT scores. We tested an SAT model with ACT participation rates, but found it did not make a difference. Therefore we concluded this analysis provides an appropriate analysis of the effects of state policy on educational outcomes.[2]

Third, we also recognized that individual-level data is more typically used to study access outcomes. However, analyses of individual databases, such as the National Longitudinal Educational

Study (NELS), could use multilevel models when the effects of state policies were examined. This approach also presents problems, given that it is not possible to use the weights with HLM.

Findings

The analyses of the impact of state policies are presented in three parts. Fixed-effects regressions for each of the three outcomes are examined below.

Student Achievement (SAT scores)
The analysis of the impact of the effects of high school reforms on student achievement reveals both demographic variables and state education policies were associated with SAT scores (Table 3). State demographic characteristics explained a substantial portion of the variance (see adjusted R^2), but SAT participation rates and high school reform do improve prediction.

Poverty rates have a negative association with SAT scores, while the percentage of other minorities in the population and percent of the population with bachelor's degrees were positively associated with the outcome across all three models. However, the coefficient for two of these variables—poverty rate and percent other minorities—dropped in significance (from .01 to .05) when state policies were considered. There is a confounding relationship between state policies and these population characteristics. States with higher poverty and lower percentages of other minority populations[3] apparently were quicker to implement some of these reform policies, an issue that should be examined further in the future.

The percentage of African Americans in the populations had a modest negative association with SAT scores before we controlled for SAT participation rates. Several of the states with high percentages of African Americans emphasize ACT exams and/or have lower percentages of high school students taking SAT exams.

Table 3. Three Step Fixed Effects for SAT Combined Score.

Variables	Step 1 - Demographic			Step 2 - Demo. & Participation Rate			Step 3 - Demo., Particip., & Policy		
	Unstand. Coeff.	Stand. Coeff.	Sig	Unstand. Coeff.	Stand. Coeff.	Sig	Unstand. Coeff.	Stand. Coeff.	Sig
% Poverty	-91.589	-0.055	***	-91.123	-0.054	***	-51.862	-0.031	**
% Black	268.472	0.486	**	130.456	0.236		152.927	0.275	
% Hispanic	56.570	0.069		100.246	0.122		-60.112	-0.074	
% Other Minorities (=Indian +Asian)	1513.939	2.072	***	1540.952	2.109	***	598.809	0.829	**
% Population w/BA or higher	1.523	0.112	***	1.595	0.117	***	1.095	0.080	***
Enrollment when the cohort was 9th grade	0.000	-0.042		0.000	-0.039		0.000	0.079	
SAT Partic. Rate				-0.532	-0.216	***	-0.264	-0.108	
Honors or advanced diploma policy							-4.126	-0.030	*
State guidelines consistent w/NCTM recomm. standards							10.083	0.067	***
% of schools partic. in AP program							0.211	0.065	**
High school exit exam required							2.676	0.020	
High (3 or 4) credits in math req. for grad							3.699	0.026	**
Local board control of math requirements for grad							-3.973	-0.020	
K-12 instructional expenditures per FTE							3.360	0.042	
Model Statistics									
Adj R^2	0.9794			0.9799			0.9831		
N	510			509			505		
P-value for F test that all $u_i=0$	0.000			0.000			0.000		

Note: *** $p<0.01$, ** $p<0.05$, * $p<0.1$

The percentage of the high school seniors who took SAT exams was negatively associated with SAT scores, an expected finding (Powell & Steelman, 1996), before the final step. Interestingly, SAT participation rates ceased to be significant when other state policies were considered. Apparently states that take action on the other policies are also states that encourage high school students to take the SAT test. This is a reasonable intermediate hypothesis, given that such an approach would be consistent with the academic access rationale described above.

Three of the state policies were statistically significant and positively associated with SAT scores. Having implemented NCTM math standards had the largest standardized beta and the strongest statistical association (.01). Both requiring three or more math courses for graduation and the percentage of high schools offering AP exams were significant and positively associated with average SAT scores.

These findings offer relatively strong support for the use of NCTM standards in math and modest support for AP courses and raising math requirements for graduation as strategies for improving test scores. However, whether the notion that requiring math courses improves access requires that we look at the other outcomes as well.

High School Graduation

The analysis of high school graduation rates (Table 4) reveals a different set of relationships for demographic variables and state education policies. There are clearly substantial differences between the ways state policies influence achievement and high school graduation rates.

A substantial part of the variance in high school graduation rates was explained by demographic differences across the states. Poverty rates were positively associated with high school graduation rates, while the percentage of other minorities and the percentage of the populations with bachelor's degrees had a negative association. Further, the significance of poverty and education level decreased when state policies were considered, indicating a relationship between population characteristics and state education policies.

Participation rates in the SAT had a modest positive association with high school graduation rates before the effects of state policies were considered. This suggests that expanding participation in college entrance exams could improve graduation rates.

Table 4. Three Step Fixed Effects Regression for High School Graduation Rate.

Variables	Step 1 - Demographic			Step 2 - Demo. & Participation Rate			Step 3 - Demo., Particip., & Policy		
	Unstand. Coeff.	Stand. Coeff.	Sig	Unstand. Coeff.	Stand. Coeff.	Sig	Unstand. Coeff.	Stand. Coeff.	Sig
% Poverty	0.212	0.092	***	0.211	0.091	***	0.144	0.063	**
% Black	0.206	0.270		0.517	0.678		0.227	0.295	
% Hispanic	-0.381	-0.336		-0.478	-0.420		-0.292	-0.259	
% Other Minorities (=Indian +Asian)	-4.285	-4.251	***	-4.351	-4.317	***	-2.592	-2.594	***
% Population w/BA or higher	-0.003	-0.146	***	-0.003	-0.154	***	-0.002	-0.097	**
Enrollment when the cohort was 9th grade	0.000	0.271		0.000	0.267		0.000	0.324	*
SAT Part. Rate				0.001	0.349	**	0.000	0.028	
Honors or advanced diploma policy							-0.001	-0.005	
State guidelines consistent w/NCTM recomm. standards							-0.015	-0.073	***
% of schools partic. in AP program							-0.002	-0.343	***
High school exit exam required							0.012	0.063	**
High (3 or 4) math credits req. for grad							-0.034	-0.176	***
Local board control of math requirements for grad							0.018	0.066	
K-12 instructional expenditures per FTE							0.022	0.196	***
Model Statistics									
Adj R^2	0.9121			0.9133			0.9266		
N	510			509			505		
P-value for F test that all u_i=0	0.000			0.000			0.000		

Note: *** $p<0.01$, ** $p<0.05$, * $p<0.1$

Other than exit exams, education policies did not improve high school graduation rates. Implementation of NCTM standards, the percentage of high schools providing AP courses, and requiring three or more math courses for high school graduation were negatively associated with graduation rates. While these policies appeared to have contributed to improvement of SAT scores (Table 3), they also were detrimental for high school graduation (Table 4).

One of the new state policies, high school exit exams, had a modest positive association with high school graduation rates, a finding that is contrary to some other studies (Jacob, 2001; Manset & Washburn, 2003). Perhaps defining a minimum threshold of achievement enables more students to graduate, controlling for other requirements they faced or the resources available.

Funding for K-12 schools was positively associated with high school graduation rates. This finding contradicts the claims of new conservative reformers who argue that funding does not make a difference in educational outcomes (Finn, 1990, 2001; Paige, 2003). While funding was not related to test scores (Table 3), it was the only policy variable with a strong positive association with high school graduation (Table 4).

When we contrast the two sets of findings it is apparent that the policies that are associated with improvement in achievement outcomes are negatively associated with high school graduation rates. The new education policies may have contributed to the modest increase in SAT scores during the 1990s, but they were also associated with the more substantial and troubling drop in graduation rates. Clearly, more balance is needed in education policy.

College Enrollment Rates

The ultimate test of efficacy of the new high school policies is whether they improve college enrollment rates for students who graduate from high school, the claim implicit in the NCES pipeline. The evidence does not support this argument (Table 5).

Two of the demographic variables were consistently associated with the outcome across the three steps. Poverty rates had a strong negative association with college enrollment rates, while percentage of other minorities in the population had a modest positive association with the outcome.

Table 5. Three Step Fixed Effects Regression for College Continuation Rate.

Variables	Step 1 - Demographic			Step 2 - Demo. & Participation Rate			Step 3 - Demo., Particip., & Policy		
	Unstand. Coeff.	Stand. Coeff.	Sig.	Unstand. Coeff.	Stand. Coeff.	Sig.	Unstand. Coeff.	Stand. Coeff.	Sig.
% Poverty	-0.573	-0.296	***	-0.570	-0.295	***	-0.525	-0.270	***
% Black	0.321	0.415		0.286	0.370		0.947	1.227	
% Hispanic	-0.407	-0.454		-0.373	-0.416		-0.093	-0.104	
% Other Minorities (=Indian +Asian)	3.104	3.883	**	3.119	3.902	**	3.525	4.428	**
% Population w/ BA or higher	0.002	0.132		0.002	0.134		0.002	0.104	
Enrollment when the cohort was 9th grade	0.000	-0.846	*	0.000	-0.834	*	0.000	-1.249	***
SAT Part. Rate				0.000	-0.174		-0.001	-0.344	
Honors or advanced diploma policy							-0.044	-0.285	***
State guidelines consistent w/ NCTM recomm. standards							-0.003	-0.017	
% of schools partic. in AP program							0.001	0.238	
High school exit exam required							0.006	0.042	
High (3 or 4) math credits req. for grad							0.017	0.107	
Local board control of math req. for grad							0.002	0.010	
K-12 instructional expenditures per FTE							-0.021	-0.235	
Model Statistics									
Adj R^2	0.7572			0.756			0.7726		
N	250			250			248		
P-value for F test that all $u_i=0$	0.000			0.000			0.000		

Note: *** $p<0.01$, ** $p<0.05$, * $p<0.1$

The size of the 9th grade cohort was negatively associated with college enrollment rates and was strongest when the state policy variables were considered. This suppressed negative association is related to the implementation of the state policies.

Only one of the policy variables had a significant association with college enrollment rates. Having honors diplomas decreased the percentage of high school graduates who went on to college. It is conceivable that making distinctions among different types of diplomas discouraged some students from pursuing college. However, it is also possible that other forces in states explain this finding.

The bottom line is that the new state education policies had little effect on college enrollment rates for students who graduate from high school and several of these policies actually decrease high school graduation rates. Therefore, there are strong compelling reasons to question the assumptions of the new conservative reformers.

Conclusions

There is little reason to doubt the research finding that high school students who take advanced math courses are more likely to enroll in college. However, building policies that are aimed at increasing the level of math achievement—successful completion of advanced classes and higher test scores—has both intended and unintended consequences. These analyses reveal that:

- A few of the new education reforms implemented in the 1990s (i.e., NCTM standards, AP courses, and requiring more math courses) had a positive association with higher SAT scores.
- Many of these new policies were also negatively associated with high school graduation rates.
- The level of funding for K-12 education was positively associated with high school graduation rates when the influence of demographic variables and state education policies were considered.
- The new education policies had little association with college enrollment rates for high school graduates.

These findings reveal the problematic nature of leaping from correlation analyses to policy initiatives. Just because a behavior—such as choosing to take an advanced math courses in high school—is associated with college enrollment, there is little reason to assume that requiring this behavior would increase college enrollment. In fact, implementing higher standards and more intensive math requirements apparently influenced the decline in high school graduation rates in the 1990s and had no impact on college enrollment rates. While advocates of these policies might claim that they had the intended effect—because in fact these policies were associated with higher SAT scores—they should also consider the unintended consequences of these policies.

More generally these results illustrate that it is critical to evaluate the effects of actual policies, rather than depending on research informed rationales. While it is probable that researchers and policymakers who advocate such leaps in policy have noble intentions, it is crucial that they also be open to contradictory evidence. Both new and contradictory evidence has emerged over time in access research. This study attempted to untangle questions related to the effects of new policies that were intended to improve student preparation for college.

The shared goals should be to improve schools so more students can qualify for college and to enable more qualified students to attend college. The research on academic preparation has informed educators about the meaning of academic qualification, but the policies that have flowed from these analyses have not adequately achieved these noble goals. The new policies have not prepared more children for college or enabled more children to go to college. Rather, these new policies appear to have enabled some children to attain higher achievement as measured by scores on standardized tests.

Notes

1. The NELS questions about college applications were asked during the senior year, which means that students answering affirmatively on these questions had applied to a college that required an advanced application. Many less selective institutions do not require students to make applications in advance.
2. We also used this model to predict ACT scores and had similar findings.
3. Since poverty had a strong negative association with SAT scores before state policies were considered, but a weaker association with

the outcome after these policies were considered, it is apparent that the high poverty (greater negative) would be mitigated by the policies. The reverse would be true for other minorities, in which case the positive effects of the variables were mitigated.

References

Adelman, C. (1999). *Answers in the tool box: Academic intensity, attendance patterns, and bachelor's degree attainment.* Washington, DC: National Center for Education Statistics.

Adelman, C. (2002). The relationship between urbanicity and educational outcomes. In W. G. Tierney & L. S. Hagedorn (Eds.), *Increasing access to college: Extending possibilities for all students.* (pp. 81-104) Albany, NY: State University of New York Press.

Advisory Committee on Student Financial Assistance. (2002). *Empty promises: The myth of college access in America.* Washington, DC: Author.

Chaikind, S. (1987). *College enrollment by black and white students.* Prepared for the U.S. Department of Education. Washington, DC: D.R.C.

Choy, S. P. (2002). *Access & persistence: Findings from 10 years of longitudinal research on students.* Washington, DC: American Council on Education.

College Entrance Examination Board. (2001). *2002 college bound seniors: A profile of SAT program test takers.* Princeton, NJ: Author.

Finn, C. E., Jr. (1990). The biggest reform of all. *Phi Delta Kappan, 71*(8), 584-92.

Finn, C. E., Jr. (2001, February 21). College isn't for everyone. *USA Today*, p. 14A.

Hansen, W. L. (1983). Impact of student aid on access. In J. Froomkin (Ed.), *The crisis in higher education* (pp. 84-96). New York: Academy of Political Science.

Jacob, B. A. (2001). Getting tough? The impact of high school graduation exams. *Educational Evaluation and Policy Analysis, 23*, 99-121.

Kramer, M. (Ed.) (1982). *Meeting student aid needs in a period of retrenchment.* New Directions in Higher Education, Vol. 4. San Francisco: Jossey-Bass.

Lefevre, A. T., & Hederman, R. S., Jr. (2001). *Report card on American education: A state-by-state analysis, 1976-2000. Washington*, DC: American Legislative Exchange Council. ERIC Document Reproduction Service No. EA031158.

Manset, G., & Washburn, S. (2003). Inclusive education in high stakes, high poverty environments: The case of students with learning disabilities in Indiana's urban high schools and the graduation qualifying examination. In L. F. Miron & E. P. St. John (Eds.), *Reinterpreting urban school reform: A critical-empirical review* (pp. 77-93). Albany: State University of New York Press.

National Center for Education Statistics. (1996). *National Education Longitudinal Study: 1988-1994, Descriptive summary report with an essay on access and choice in postsecondary education.* NCES 96-175. Washington, DC: Author.

National Center for Education Statistics. (1997a). *Access to higher postsecondary education for the 1992 high school graduates,* NCES 98-105. By Lutz Berkner & Lisa Chavez. Project Officer: C. Dennis Carroll. Washington, DC: Author.

National Center for Education Statistics. (1997b). *Confronting the odds: Students at risk and the pipeline to higher education.* NCES 98-094. By Laura J. Horn. Project officer: C. Dennis Carroll. Washington, DC: Author.

National Center for Education Statistics. (2000). *Mapping the road to college: First-generation students' math track, planning strategies, and context of support.* NCES 2000-153. By Laura Horn & Anne-Marie Nunez. Project Officer: Larry Bobbitt. Washington, DC: Author.

National Center for Education Statistics. (2002). *The condition of education.* By John Wirt, Susan Choy, Debra Gerald, Stephen Provasnik, Patrick Rooney, Satoshi Watanabe, & Richard Tobin. Washington, DC: Author.

Paige, R. (2003, Jan. 10). More spending is not the answer. Opposing view: Improving quality of schools calls for high standards, accountability. *USA Today,* p. 11A.

Pelavin, S. H., & Kane, M. B. (1988). *Minority participation in higher education.* Washington, DC: Pelavin Associates.

Pelavin, S. H., & Kane, M. B. (1990). *Changing the odds: Factors increasing access to college.* New York: College Board.

Powell, B., & Steelman, L. C. (1996). Bewitched, bothered, and bewildering: The use and misuse of state SAT and ACT rankings. *Harvard Educational Review, 66*(1), 27-59.

St. John, E. P. (2003). *Refinancing the college dream: Access, equal opportunity, and justice for taxpayers.* Baltimore: Johns Hopkins University Press.

St. John, E. P. (in press). Policy research and political decisions. In E. P. St. John & M. D. Parsons (Eds.), *Public Funding for Higher Education: New Contexts, New Rationales.* Baltimore: Johns Hopkins University Press .

St. John, E. P., & Byce, C. (1982). The changing federal role in student financial aid. In M. Kramer (Ed.), *Meeting student aid needs in a period of retrenchment,* New directions in higher education, Vol. 40, (pp. 21-40). San Francisco: Jossey-Bass.

Wilson, R. (1986). *Overview of the issue: Minority/poverty student enrollment problems.* Paper presented at the NASSG/NCHELP Conference on Student Financial Aid Research, Third Annual in Chicago, IL.

CHAPTER 8

POSTSECONDARY ENCOURAGEMENT FOR DIVERSE STUDENTS: A REEXAMINATION OF THE TWENTY-FIRST CENTURY SCHOLARS PROGRAM

Glenda D. Musoba[1]

While the rate of college enrollment by high school graduates was nearly equal across ethnic groups in the late 1970s when Pell grants were more adequate, since the 1980s Hispanic and African American students have participated in higher education at lower rates than Whites or Asian Americans (St. John 2002, 2003; Terenzini, Cabrera, & Bernal, 2001). As the gross number of students from underrepresented minorities in higher education increased in recent decades, their participation has become inequitable in relation to their representation in the college age population of high school graduates (St. John, 2002). This new inequality is even more problematic because the percentage of minorities in the overall population increased since 1980. Similarly, low-income students attend higher education at a lower rate than high-income students, even when controlling for academic ability.

In the current political climate, it is highly unlikely the federal government will take the substantial steps necessary to provide sufficient grant aid to equalize access between income and ethnic groups. The federal Pell grant program has not kept pace with tuition increases. Further, many states failed to increase grant aid as tuition rose when institutional subsidies from states declined.

States provide a useful unit of analysis for understanding and examining programs and policies to increase access. In recent years, some states have followed the model of the Georgia Hope Scholarship program and have increased merit-based aid. While these programs may be politically popular, preliminary analyses suggest they do little to increase the college-going rate of the lowest-income students (Heller, Chapter 5). Other states, while they allowed tuition to increase, provided more substantial need-based grant aid. A third approach is to focus state efforts on changes in academic policy to increase college participation (St. John, et al., Chapter 7). A fourth approach involves the creation of early intervention to encourage participation in higher education (Tierney & Hagedorn, 2002). If coupled with adequate grant aid, early encouragement has potential in overcoming the access gap (St. John, Musoba, Simmons & Chung, 2002). Since these programs may affect majority and minority students differently, it is important to study the distinct impact of these programs on diverse groups of students. To fail to do so could result in applying policies that are based on understandings from research on majority students, but such policies could have a detrimental impact on minority students. Further study of early intervention and grant programs by ethnicity is needed.

Indiana provides a useful case study of a state intervention program to increase college participation. Indiana's Twenty-first Century Scholars Program combines early postsecondary encouragement with adequate grant aid for low-income seventh or eighth grade students who promise to prepare for college. Prior research has demonstrated the overall effectiveness of this program (St. John, Musoba, Simmons, & Chung, 2002), but an analysis by ethnicity will add to our understanding of access. This chapter summarizes key features of postsecondary access programs.

Background

Aspirations for postsecondary education are high among all young people. Analysis of the National Education Longitudinal Study (NLES, 88) indicate that over 94 percent of all eighth graders in the 1988 sample who later finish high school plan to attend postsecondary education at some point in their lives regardless of ethnicity or family income (National Center for Education Statistics [NCES], 1997a). When the question was changed to read "attend directly after high school," it was still 70 percent for the lowest-income students and 68 percent and 77 percent for Latino/a (hereafter Latino) and African American students respectively. The Stanford University's Bridge Project revealed that 88 percent of all students and over 80 percent of African American and Latino students plan to attend some form of postsecondary education (Venezia, Kierst, & Antonio, 2003). Clearly, students' aspirations to attend higher education are high regardless of income and ethnic groups, yet gaps exist in participation related to family socioeconomic status and ethnicity (Mortensen, 2001, 2002; NCES, 1997a, 1997b, 2000, 2001, 2002; St. John, 2002).

Low participation by low-income and minority students is in part due to inadequate financial aid (Advisory Committee on Student Financial Assistance, 2002). Federal Pell grants have not kept pace with increases in college tuition. In 1975-76, the maximum Pell grant covered 85 percent of the average cost of attendance; but in the 1999-2000 school year, Pell grants covered only 39 percent of the costs (St. John, 2003). The federal government has shifted its emphasis from grant aid to loan aid and tax credits in recent years. More recent policy decisions have focused on the middle-income rather than low-income students, somewhat abandoning the original philosophical base for politically expedient policies. Tax credits implemented during the 1990s subtract Pell awards from the credit, therefore excluding the lowest-income families.

A series of studies on financial access suggests students' college choice process is impacted by financial factors as well as aspirations and academic performance. Early analyses by St. John and Noell (1989) found African American students were more responsive to grant aid while White students were more responsive to loan aid when making the choice to enroll in college. More recently, St. John, Paulsen, and Starkey (1996) proposed a financial nexus model which suggests a series of decision points to choose, enroll, and persist in college based on family financial circumstances and other factors. In the first stage, students' family circumstances and academic abilities influence their perceptions of their ability to pay for college and their college planning. In the second stage, students engage in a cost benefit analysis which influences the institution they select and their commitment to enroll and later persist. The students' perceptions about their families' financial situation can determine their college choice. For instance, a student concerned about costs is more likely to choose an institution because of low tuition. Finally, in the third stage, the fit between the student (and as the students' degree of academic success) and the institutional characteristics are part of the students' ongoing cost benefit analysis in the choice to persist. A distinctive feature of the nexus model is the importance of the indirect or intangible nature of the influence of finances on the college choice and persistence process.

In further research Paulsen and St. John (2002) found low-income students were most negatively affected by grant inadequacy, while working class students in the next tier were more conscious about employment while enrolling. Paulsen and St. John also maintained that income and ethnicity are not synonymous in the choice and enrollment process. For instance, poor and working class African American students were more likely to persist than their White peers of similar income, while low-income Asian American students were less likely to persist. Paulsen, St. John, and Carter (2002) completed the most recent analyses. They found African Americans were the most financially sensitive, with grant aid being most important, similar to low-income students in the Paulsen and St. John study. Latino students were also concerned about costs but behaved in working-class patterns with strong concerns about loan debt and employment while in college. Finally, White students appeared to benefit most from current federal aid policy, which emphasizes loans and tax credits over grants.

Several conclusions relevant to the current discussion can be drawn from this line of research. Clearly students' enrollment choices are influenced by financial need, and these choices are situated in the context of their family and cultural backgrounds. Further, financial aid is important to access for minority students, and policies that do not consider ethnicity may have unintended consequences that favor some students over others.

In addition to recent financial access research, a separate but parallel line of research on postsecondary encouragement programs designed to increase access has also developed. Federal and state funds for GEAR UP and other programs focus on enhancing access through helping students aspire to college and prepare academically. After school, summer, and tutoring programs are all examples of ways programs address academic preparation. TRIO and other early preparation programs provide postsecondary encouragement with campus visits, career counseling, and mentoring. Research on postsecondary encouragement programs is limited and lacks rigor (Tierney & Hagedorn, 2002), yet providing information about college options and financial aid can raise student aspirations for college (Hossler, Schmit, & Vesper, 1999). Tierney and Hagedorn (2002) identify a number of features of effective postsecondary preparation programs. These include an emphasis on academics, parental involvement, strong connections with postsecondary institutions, stable financial support for the program, preparation of students for a variety of postsecondary options, and early intervention.

Comprehensive early intervention programs are designed to improve access for low-income and minority students. Sound policies and programs to enhance postsecondary access must be just. Programs must make efficient use of taxpayer dollars yet be sufficient to have their desired impact on college enrollment, and must be effective for all student populations.

While many programs may have a positive impact, ideally, comprehensive and sufficient means a program addresses all three aspects of access: academic preparation, postsecondary encouragement, and financial need. Programs that prepare students who cannot afford to attend will be limited in their effectiveness. Similarly, financial access for students who have not taken a college preparatory curriculum means remedial coursework and extra time to reach their goals. Finally, when low-income students with high grades do not aspire to attend at rates similar to high-income students (St. John, Paulsen, & Carter, 2002), programs must provide information about career options and encouragement to attend higher education. The question remaining asks: what do comprehensive early intervention programs need to do to better improve minority access? A case study of Indiana's Twenty-first Century Scholars Program may provide some additional insights.

Indiana's Twenty-first Century Scholars Program
In the 1990s, Indiana made substantial progress in raising the number of high school graduates who go to college (Mortensen,

2000). Several policy changes were likely attributed to this success, including the Twenty-first Century Scholars Program. All seventh or eighth graders who meet the income guidelines to be eligible for free or reduced lunch are invited to enroll in the Scholars program. Enrollment in the program forms a contract between the student and the state. The student agrees to graduate from high school with a 2.0 grade point average, apply for financial aid and college admission, demonstrate good citizenship by remaining drug- and alcohol-free and refraining from committing a crime, and enroll in college within two years of high school graduation. In return, the state promises to pay the full tuition costs at an Indiana public college or a comparable amount at a private college. This aid fills the gap between state need-based aid and the full tuition costs at a public institution. In addition, the state provides support services, including campus visits, workshops on financial aid, information about a college preparatory curriculum, tutoring, test preparation, mentoring, and parent workshops. The program encourages students to take a rigorous academic program and provides supplementary grant aid. Students enroll in the program during their seventh or eighth grade of school; therefore, intervention begins early. Students affirm their enrollment by applying for financial aid during their senior year of high school. Students choose which, if any, support services they attend, but at a minimum receive regular mailings on college access topics.

Prior analyses of the Twenty-first Century Scholars Program found that the early encouragement combined with grant aid improved the college participation rate of low-income students (St. John, Musoba, Simmons, Chung, Schmit, & Peng, in press). The study also tested the success of the program for students in high-poverty schools and found that Scholars in those environments were also more likely to attend college than their peers.[2] Therefore, the program is effective overall, but it is also important to examine how this and similar programs might have a differential impact on students from different ethnic groups, particularly underrepresented minority students. Students may respond to policies and circumstances differently depending on their life experience. Therefore, we asked: does a college access program such as the Twenty-first Century Scholars Program improve the college-going rates of both White and African American students? Through the Scholars Program, we can examine the relationship between college attendance, student background, academic experience, and state policy for the two student groups.

Methods

Database

For this analysis, we used a cohort of Indiana high school students who were on track to graduate from high school in 1999 when they completed a student survey four years prior in 9th grade. The survey questions included items regarding aspirations for college, home environment, school achievement in 9th grade, and parent education. This ninth-grade survey data was merged with the Indiana public college data for the 1999-2000 school year, therefore adding college attendance information. We estimated attendance for students who applied for aid listing an out-of-state or a private college in Indiana based on their financial aid awards or applications. In the matched data, there were 65,335 usable cases; 46,225 were White, 4,278 were African American, and the remainder were other races with no sample large enough to test.

Statistical Method

Multilevel modeling, using HLM software, was used because of the nested nature of the data. Both student- and school-level variables were used in the analyses. Multilevel modeling takes into account the lack of independence of the cases. Two sets of multilevel logistic regression analyses for White and African American students were completed to assess the effect of the Scholars Program. While the analyses are parallel, coefficient size cannot be compared between the models because they are separate analyses.

The first pair of analyses examined the impact of taking the Scholar's pledge in eighth grade on taking the steps to prepare for college by applying for financial aid. The second set of analyses examined the relationship between being a Scholar in the twelfth grade who affirmed the Scholarship by applying for financial aid and enrolling in college the following fall.

Regression Models

Two levels of variables were considered in the models.

Student demographic and academic variables known to be associated with college enrollment were entered. These included:

- Gender,
- Parent education (parents who had graduated from college were compared to parents with less education),
- Family structure (students from two-parent homes were compared to one-parent or no-parent homes) and home language (students from primarily English speaking homes were compared to those from families that primarily spoke another language),
- Prior academic achievement (students who earned mostly B grades were compared to students who earned mostly A grades and students who earned grades lower than B's,
- Educational aspirations (students who aspired to a four-year college degree or higher were compared to groups of students who aspired to less: two-year degree, less than a two-year degree, and high school diploma or less),
- Twenty-first Century Scholarship status (students who had taken the pledge in eighth grade were compared to all other students for the preparation for college analyses and students who affirmed the pledge in twelfth grade were compared to all other students for the enrollment analyses).

School was the second level of the multilevel model. School-level variables provided a measure of the high school context within which students made their choices. School variables included:

- Locale of the high school (urban or rural compared to suburban, town, or unknown),
- Percent minority (a dichotomous variable for either a high or low percentage of minority students in the high school),
- Percent of the graduates who earn Honors diplomas[3] (a dichotomous variable for either a high or low percentage of Honors graduates in the students' graduating classes) provided a measure of the academic or competitive rigor of the high school,

- Extent of poverty (a design set of variables dividing students into quartiles and comparing students from the three poorer quartiles of schools to students in the highest average income high schools, based on the percent of students in the school eligible for free or reduced lunches) provided a measure of the students' peer income group.

Two regressions were run for African American students and two for White students. In the first analyses, the outcome was a dichotomous measure of whether the student took the steps to prepare for college by applying for financial aid, therefore affirming their scholarship for the Scholars in the sample. In the second set of analyses, whether or not the student enrolled in college either full- or part-time in the fall of 1999 was the outcome variable.

Limitations
The study limitations relate to the structure and complexities of the database. We consider the critical limitations below. First, we lacked an ideal comparison group. The data provided no measure of student family income in 8th or 9th grade (or ever, for many cases). The best comparison group for Scholars would be students who were also low-income in 8th grade and did not enroll in the program. Therefore, Scholars who are all low-income are being compared to students from all economic backgrounds. We also cannot control for the self-selection factor, in that some students chose to enroll in the program and other eligible students did not. Nearly half of low-income middle school students do not take the steps to prepare for college (NCES, 1997a, St. John, 2002). Many simply drop out before their peers graduate high school. So the lack of an appropriate comparison group should be taken into account in all access studies that examine low-income populations.

This lack of information on family income and whether students were eligible for student aid meant we lacked the data needed to simulate the probability of applying for the program, a method used in several recent econometric studies (Kane, 2003; van der Klaauw, 2002). This limitation could bias our estimates of the impact of the Scholars Program on aid application, our indication of meeting program requirements.

Second, our information on college enrollment was inconsistent across groups. For the Scholars and other financial aid applicants who enrolled in public institutions in state we had information on enrollment from the state's student information system. We could also discern whether recipients of financial aid attended a private college in state because of records maintained by the State Student Assistance Commission of Indiana (SSACI). To adjust for this limitation, we assumed that aid applicants who applied to an out-of-state college or in-state private college and who did not enroll in a public college in Indiana enrolled in a college out of state or a private college. We think this was a reasonable assumption because most students who go out of state or to private colleges have some financial need and most colleges that award merit or need-based scholarships require students to fill out the FAFSA. However, there may be a few high-income students who enrolled in out-of-state colleges or in-state private colleges and made no financial aid application or students who applied for aid out-of-state but chose not to go anywhere.

Third, we lacked data on high school courses taken by students and on high school grades. We included a data element on the percentage of Honors diplomas awarded in the high school as a way of assessing the impact of variability in high school contexts. Therefore, our analyses do not fully assess the impact of taking a college preparatory curriculum, but they do estimate the influence of high school contexts on access.

Finally, there may be other minor incentives besides concerns about college costs to enroll in the Scholars Program. For example, students may desire the additional support of the program and parents may appreciate the extra incentive for their children to refrain from drug use. However, the primary benefit of the program is the tuition grant and the grant was what was promoted to prospective students.

Findings

Description of students

Students in the high school class of 1999 who took the pledge to be Scholars in the 8th grade comprised only 5.46 percent of the student sample, and more than half of these students (3.43 percent) became affirmed Scholars in 12th grade. Of the White sample, 4.4 percent enrolled in the Scholars Program, but 13.6 percent of the African American sample enrolled (see Table 1). While 35.7

percent of White students' parents went to college, only 30.6 percent of African American students had parents with a college education.

Table 1. Descriptive Statistics for Variables in the Logistic Regression.

Variables	All cases/all 9th graders	White students	Black students
	Percent	Percent	Percent
Non-scholars:	94.6	97.3	90.4
8th gr. Twenty-first Century Scholar enrollee	5.4	4.4	13.6
12th gr. Twenty-first Century Scholar who took the steps to prepare	3.4	2.7	9.6
Female	48.2	50.4	50.4
Male or did not answer	51.8	49.6	49.6
White	70.4		
African American/Black	6.6		
Other minority	6.3		
Unknown ethnicity/ did not answer	16.7		
Parents did not go to college	68.4	64.3	69.4
Parents went to college	31.6	35.7	30.6
Student lives with both parents	78.7	80.8	46.9
Live with one parent	18.3	16.9	44.0
Do not live with parent	3.0	2.3	9.1
English is the home language	98.9	99.6	98.7
Spanish or other language spoken at home	1.1	0.4	1.3
Mostly A's	10.1	12.2	2.9
Mixed A's and B's and mostly B's	39.6	45.0	28.7
Mixed B's and C's and Mostly C's	33.8	32.4	47.9
Mixed C's and D's and lower	10.7	9.2	17.8
GPA unavailable	5.9	1.2	2.7
Undecided aspirations	17.6	12.8	11.5
Aspire to a high school diploma or less	7.9	7.0	10.0
Aspire to less than a 2 year degree	5.6	5.5	8.2
Aspire to a 2 year degree	7.9	7.8	9.6
Aspired to a four-year degree or higher	60.9	66.9	60.7
Students from h. s.'s in suburban locales or large or small towns	78.8	76.6	91.3
Urban-large city locale for h.s.	2.3	1.5	7.7

Table 1. Descriptive Statistics for Variables in the Logistic Regression. (Continued)

Variables	All cases/all 9th graders	White students	Black students
	Percent	Percent	Percent
Rural locale for h.s	18.9	21.9	1.0
Mean % Honors diplomas in high school	20.9	21.9	13.7
Mean % minority students in the h.s.	13.4	8.8	54.5
Lowest quartile % of students on free lunch in h.s.	24.6	28.2	4.1
Low-middle quartile % free lunch in h.s.	25.7	27.6	9.0
High-middle quartile % free lunch in h.s.	24.2	24.8	11.9
Highest quartile % free lunch in h.s.	25.4	19.4	75.0
Did not apply for financial aid	47.7	46.1	43.1
Applied for financial aid	52.3	53.9	56.9
Did not enroll in higher education	43.2	40.4	46.6
Enrolled in higher education	56.8	59.6	53.4
Level 1 N	65,335	46,225	4,278
Level 2 N	378	369	175

Middle school grades were slightly lower for African American students, as were aspirations to higher education. While 67 percent of White students aspired to a four-year college degree or higher, only 61 percent of African Americans had similar aspirations. African American students lived in more suburban or urban locales, while 22 percent of White students lived in rural areas. White students were more likely to attend high schools with high percentages of students receiving Honors diplomas. African American students went to more diverse high schools.

For White students the average percent of minority students attending their school was 9 percent while for African American students it was 55 percent. While White students were more evenly distributed across the schools on the measure of poverty, 75 percent of African American students were clustered in the schools categorized as high-poverty because of the percent of students who were eligible for free or reduced price lunches in the school. In comparing the outcome variables, 60 percent of White students attended college in the fall of 1999 while 53 percent of African American students attended. A closer percentage of White and African American students applied for aid with 54 percent of Whites and 57 percent of African American students applying.

Impact of Scholars' Pledge To Take Steps to Prepare for College

The impact of the Scholars Program and other variables on whether students took the steps to prepare for college by applying for financial aid was examined separately for White and African American students. For White students, both the individual-level and school-level variables were significant (middle columns in Table 2). Enrolling in the Twenty-first Century Scholars Program in eighth grade increased the odds that a White student would apply for financial aid. Several NCES (1997) reports emphasize the importance of applying for aid as one of the necessary steps students take to prepare and as a predictor of future college enrollment. Further, a timely aid application ensures students will be eligible for the maximum assistance. The Scholars Program increases the likelihood that a White student would apply for financial aid.

Several student background variables were also significant for White students. White males were less likely to apply for aid as were students who did not live with their parents; however, there was no significant difference between one- and two-parent homes. Students whose parents graduated from college were less likely to apply for aid, but this may be an artifact of the higher family earning power of the degree.

Students' educational experiences were also important. Students with A grades were more likely to apply for aid than B students, while students with lower grades were less likely to apply. This may also be related to their likelihood of attending or it may be that students with higher grades are given better information regarding the college admissions process in their high schools. White students who aspired to less than a four-year degree were less likely to apply for aid, including students who aspired to a two-year degree. This is consistent with prior research that community college students are less likely to apply for financial aid (Grubb & Tuma, 1991).

Several school-level variables were significant for White students, meaning they do influence individual students to apply for aid. Urban and rural students were more likely to apply for aid, which is consistent with income distribution in society. Students from high schools with higher percentages of minority students were less likely to take the steps to prepare for college by applying for aid. Students from higher-poverty schools were more likely to apply for financial aid than students from the highest average family income group.

There were some similarities and some differences from White students in the individual level variables for African American students (right columns in Table 2). Similar to White students, African American Twenty-first Century Scholars were more likely to apply for financial aid than non-Scholars. This indicates that for African American students the Scholars Program encouraged them to take the steps to prepare for college.

There were several significant student background variables. African American males were less likely to apply for financial aid than females, and students whose home language was not English were less likely to apply. There was no significant difference among African American students based on their parents' education. This may suggest that for African American parents a college degree does not offer quite the same earning power as for White parents, or it may be that parent education is not the strong predictor of taking the steps to prepare for college for African American students that it is for majority students. Similar to White students, African American students who did not live with two parents were less likely to apply for aid, while there was no significant difference between one- and two-parent homes.

Students' academic experience was important for African American students. Students who had A grades in middle school were more likely to apply for aid than B students, while students who earned lower than B grades were less likely to apply. As with White students, it may be that African American students with lower early achievement internalized the message that higher education is not for them.

African American students who did not aspire to a college degree were less likely to apply for aid than students who aspired to a four-year degree. However, unlike White students, there was no significant difference between students who aspire to a two-year degree or to a four-year degree or higher.

The level-two variables in the model for African American students were not statistically significant at a .05 level (see right columns in Table 2). Two possible explanations are offered here. First, it should be noted that the smaller sample size and the demographic nature of race in America made for a more restricted range in the variables. For instance, while White students were relatively evenly distributed among the schools, a full 75 percent of African Americans were clustered in high-poverty schools. The alternative explanation might be that school-level factors have less of an impact on African American students.

Table 2: The Impact of Enrolling in the Scholars Program in Eighth Grade on Applying for Aid and Affirming the Scholarship Enrollment: HGLM Regression Analyses of Aid Application for White and African American Students.

	White Students				African American Students			
	Coeff.	Std. Err.	Odds Rat	Sig	Coeff.	Std. Err.	Odds Rat	Sig
Student Level Variables								
21st-Century Scholar: Affirmed (Gr. 12)	0.24	0.05	1.28	***	0.43	0.10	1.54	***
Gender: Male	-0.14	0.02	0.87	***	-0.34	0.07	0.71	***
Parent Education: College Graduate	-0.10	0.02	0.91	***	-0.04	0.07	0.96	NS
Family Structure:								
One parent	-0.01	0.03	0.99	NS	-0.08	0.07	0.93	NS
No parents	-0.30	0.07	0.74	***	-0.32	0.12	0.73	**
Home Language: Spanish or other lang.	-0.29	0.15	0.75	NS	-0.89	0.31	0.41	**
Grades in 8th Grade:								
Mostly A's	0.44	0.03	1.55	***	0.58	0.23	1.79	*
Mixed B's/C's or Mostly C's	-0.65	0.02	0.52	***	-0.45	0.08	0.64	***
C's and Below	-0.94	0.04	0.39	***	-0.74	0.10	0.48	***
No GPA Reported	-0.58	0.09	0.56	***	-0.73	0.21	0.48	***
Aspirations for after college:								
High school diploma or less	-0.68	0.04	0.51	***	-0.49	0.11	0.61	***
Less than a 2 year	-0.53	0.05	0.59	***	-0.45	0.12	0.64	***
2 year degree	-0.30	0.04	0.74	***	-0.21	0.11	0.81	NS
Undecided	-0.33	0.03	0.72	***	-0.30	0.11	0.74	**

Table 2: The Impact of Enrolling in the Scholars Program in Eighth Grade on Applying for Aid and Affirming the Scholarship Enrollment: HGLM Regression Analyses of Aid Application for White and African American Students. (Continued)

	White Students				African American Students			
	Coeff.	Std. Err.	Odds Rat	Sig	Coeff.	Std. Err.	Odds Rat	Sig
School Level Variables								
H. S. Locale								
Urban-large city	0.26	0.13	1.30	*	-0.09	0.16	0.91	NS
Rural	0.10	0.04	1.10	**	0.14	0.34	1.15	NS
H. S. Characteristics								
Pct. Honors Dip	0.00	0.00	1.00	NS	0.00	0.01	1.00	NS
Pct. Minority	-0.64	0.15	0.53	***	0.38	0.20	1.47	NS
H. S. Poverty								
Low-middle poverty	0.20	0.04	1.22	***	0.00	0.21	1.00	NS
High-middle	0.16	0.04	1.17	***	-0.09	0.20	0.92	NS
Highest poverty	0.16	0.05	1.18	**	-0.09	0.19	0.91	NS
White student model random effects (Variance components)	SD	Variance	df		X^2			p
Intercept	0.199	0.040	361		774.500			0.000
Black student model random effects (Variance components)	SD	Variance	df		X^2			p
Intercept	0.174	0.030	167		195.534			0.065

*** $p < .001$, ** $p < .01$, * $p < .05$

Impact of Affirmed Scholars Enrollment on College Enrollment

The impact of the Scholars Program and other variables on college enrollment for White and African American students was examined separately (Table 3). For White students, both individual-level and school-level variables were significantly related to college enrollment (middle columns in Table 3).

Being an affirmed Scholar had the largest impact on college enrollment of the variables considered in the model. White scholars were four times more likely to enroll in college than non-Scholars, controlling for other factors.

Several student demographic characteristics were significant. White males were less likely to enroll than females. Parent education was significant and positive. Having parents who attended college increased the chance of college enrollment by 1.24 times. Living in a different family structure from a two-parent home decreased the odds of enrolling in college as did speaking a language other than English in the home.

Students' school experiences were also noteworthy. Middle school grades that were mostly A's were associated with a greater chance of enrollment; grades below B were associated with a lower chance of enrollment. Students who aspired to anything less than a four-year degree had a lower probability of college enrollment, including aspiring to a two-year degree.

A number of school-level variables were not significantly related to college enrollment for White students, but several significant variables merit discussion. The percent of students earning an Honors diploma in the student's high school was positively associated with going to college, suggesting a rigorous academic environment may be important for White students. Attending high-poverty schools was negatively associated with college enrollment for White students. This is consistent with prior research regarding the negative effects of income segregation across schools.

The analysis of college going for African American students (right columns in Table 3) has several interesting differences from the White analysis as well as some similar patterns. Being an affirmed Scholar was significantly associated with college enrollment. African American Scholars were six times more likely to enroll in college than non-Scholars, controlling for other factors.

Table 3. The Impact of Being an Affirmed Scholar (Applying for Aid in Grade 12) on College Enrollment: HGLM Regression Analyses of College Enrollment for White and African American Students.

	White Students				African American Students			
	Coeff.	Std. Err.	Odds Rat	Sig	Coeff.	Std. Err.	Odds Rat	Sig
Student Level Variables								
21st-Century Scholar: Affirmed (Gr. 12)	1.44	0.08	4.23	***	1.83	0.16	6.26	***
Gender: Male	-0.13	0.02	0.88	***	-0.21	0.07	0.81	**
Parent Education: College Graduate	0.22	0.02	1.24	***	-0.02	0.07	0.98	NS
Family Structure:								
One parent in Home	-0.18	0.03	0.83	***	-0.19	0.07	0.83	**
No parents in Home	-0.43	0.07	0.65	***	-0.34	0.12	0.71	**
Home Language: Spanish or other lang.	-0.48	0.16	0.62	**	-0.73	0.31	0.48	*
Grades in 8th Grade								
Mostly A's	0.32	0.04	1.37	***	0.34	0.22	1.40	NS
Mixed B's/C's or Mostly C's	-0.72	0.02	0.49	***	-0.46	0.08	0.63	***
C's and Below	-1.02	0.04	0.36	***	-0.68	0.11	0.51	***
No GPA Reported	-0.65	0.09	0.52	***	-1.06	0.22	0.35	***
Aspirations for after college								
High school diploma or less	-0.72	0.04	0.49	***	-0.44	0.12	0.64	***
Less than a 2 year	-0.61	0.05	0.55	***	-0.39	0.12	0.68	**
2 year degree	-0.47	0.04	0.62	***	-0.18	0.11	0.84	NS
Undecided	-0.43	0.03	0.65	***	-0.34	0.11	0.71	**

Table 3. The Impact of Being an Affirmed Scholar (Applying for Aid in Grade 12) on College Enrollment: HGLM Regression Analyses of College Enrollment for White and African American Students. (Continued)

	White Students				African American Students			
	Coeff.	Std. Err.	Odds Rat	Sig	Coeff.	Std. Err.	Odds Rat	Sig
School Level Variables								
H. S. Locale:								
Urban-large city	-0.12	0.14	0.89	NS	-0.14	0.17	0.87	NS
Rural	-0.01	0.04	0.99	NS	-0.10	0.35	0.91	NS
H. S. Characteristics:								
Pct. Honors Dip	0.01	0.00	1.01	***	0.01	0.01	1.01	NS
Pct. Minority	-0.16	0.17	0.85	NS	0.39	0.21	1.48	NS
H. S. Poverty								
Low-middle poverty	0.01	0.05	1.01	NS	-0.08	0.22	0.93	NS
High-middle	-0.11	0.05	0.90	*	-0.27	0.21	0.76	NS
Highest poverty	-0.26	0.06	0.77	***	-0.43	0.20	0.65	*
White student model random effects (Variance components)	SD	Variance	df		X^2	p		
Intercept	0.243	0.059	361		915.786	0.000		
Black student model random effects (Variance components)	SD	Variance	df		X^2	p		
Intercept	0.201	0.040	167		192.402	0.087		

*** $p<.001$, ** $p<.01$, * $p<.05$

Numerous student background variables were significant. African American males were less likely to enroll than females. Living in a single parent home or living away from parents were negatively associated with college enrollment as was living in a home where English was not the primary language. Unlike in the analysis of White students, parent education was not significantly related to college enrollment for African American students. This non-significance is particularly important in light of the strong emphasis that NCES (Choy, 2002; NCES, 1997) has placed on parent education. It is important to consider whether a general analysis of all students means researchers are applying results dominated by White students to minority students.

There were also differences between White and African American students related to students' academic experiences and aspirations. While low grades were negatively associated with college enrollment, there was no significant difference between A and B grades for African American students. African Americans who earn B grades are as likely to go to college as African American students who earn A grades.

Aspiring to less than a two-year degree or being undecided about college plans was negatively associated with college enrollment, but there was no significant difference between aspirations for a two-year or four-year degree for African American students. Considering minority students are more likely than White students to start their education in a community college, this is important. It also suggests that in future analyses of college access for African American students, it is important to not limit the analyses to four-year colleges.

The level-two variables in the model for African American students were not statistically significant using a .05 level (see right column in Table 3). However, when using a less restrictive .1 criteria, one notes that students in the highest-poverty schools were less likely to enroll in college than students in the wealthiest fourth of schools. As a rough measure of income, this suggests further research is needed on the adequacy of aid. In this model there were controls for prior achievement, aspirations, etc., but this basic measure of family income suggests that financial need still hinders the poorest students.

Conclusions

By separating the racial groups we were able to see the relationships between individual-level variables and college going were different between White and African American students in some important ways. Parent education was not significant for African American students but was significant for White students. This calls into question the importance of parent education for the education path of African American students. Considering the weight some reports place on parent education, this should be explored further. Results for the majority population should not automatically be assumed to be true for minority students as well. African American Scholars were six times more likely to enroll in college than non-Scholars, while White Scholars were four times more likely. Considering that African American students generally attend lower quality high schools (Haycock, 1998) and attend college at lower rates than White students, postsecondary encouragement programs, such as the Scholars Program, that include adequate financial aid and information about colleges, are important factors in equalizing access between racial groups.

Future research on college access must continue to consider both academic and financial access. While this analysis does not completely separate the impact of aspects of the program, i.e., financial aid, academic preparation, and postsecondary encouragement, it does demonstrate that a program that combines all three is effective in increasing college enrollment for majority and minority students. The first step in this study examined the role of the Twenty-first Century Scholars Program in postsecondary encouragement and preparation, while the second step measured the direct effects of the grant. The program proved to have a measurable association in both processes. States that offer postsecondary encouragement or focus their efforts at reforming academic preparation without also providing financial aid to academically prepared low-income students are preparing students for disappointment.

This study demonstrates that encouragement combined with adequate aid is effective in increasing college access for low-income African American and White students. Encouragement services enhance aspirations and help students academically prepare for college. Students who see college as feasible for them are more likely to take the steps to prepare, as was demonstrated in the aid application analysis. The grant dollars in the Scholarship make college possible for low-income students to attend. While all students in the Scholars Program were by definition low-income, the regression analyses demonstrated that the Scholars grants do increase enrollment. State policies that match encouragement services with grant aid are more likely to be successful.

Yet, states and programs must also take the steps to reach out to students and communities that are underrepresented in higher education. While the Scholar's Program is having positive results, more urban and rural students could and should be served by the Program. Students from communities where few students consider college need extra support.

Notes

1. Ed St. John, Ada Simmons, Chong-Geun Chung, and Joanne Peng provided guidance in the implementation of the study. Ed St. John was particularly helpful in design of the model and draft reviews. Stan Jones, Jeff Weber, Jack Schmidt, Hong Zhang, and Nick Vesper provided student data. This support is sincerely appreciated. The opinions expressed in the paper are the authors' and do not represent official policies or positions of Lumina Foundation or the other agencies and individuals that supported the project.
2. Non-scholars from high-poverty schools provided the best available comparison group of low-income students for Scholars who are all, by definition, low-income. Family income in the eighth grade was not available in the data; therefore students from high-poverty schools provided an alternative reference group to all public school students.
3. The State of Indiana requires high schools to offer both a Core 40 diploma (general college preparatory) and an Honors diploma (extra courses in math, English, science, and foreign language).

References

Advisory Committee on Student Financial Assistance. (2002). *Empty promises: The myth of college access in America.* Washington, DC: Author.

Choy, S. (2002). *Access and persistence: Findings from 10 years of longitudinal research on students.* Washington, DC: American Council on Education.

Grubb, W. N., & Tuma, J. (1991). Who gets student aid? Variations in access to aid. *Review of Higher Education, 14*(3), 359-381.

Haycock, K. (1998). Good teaching matters: How well-qualified teachers can close the gap. *Thinking K-16, 3*(2).

Heller, D., & Marin, P. (2002). *Who should we help? The negative social consequences of merit scholarships.* The Civil Rights Project, Harvard University. Retrieved from http://www.civilrightsproject.harvard.edu/research/meritaid/call_merit02.php

Hossler, D., Schmit, J., & Vesper, N. (1999). *Going to college.* Baltimore: Johns Hopkins University Press.

Kane, T. (2003). *A quasi-experimental estimate of the impact of financial aid on college-going.* NBER Working Paper No. W9703 May.

National Center for Education Statistics. (1997a). *Access to higher postsecondary education for the 1992 high school graduates.* NCES 98-105. By Lutz Berkner & Lisa Chavez. Project Officer: C. Dennis Carroll. Washington, DC: Author.

National Center for Education Statistics. (1997b). *Confronting the odds: Students at risk and the pipeline to higher education.* NCES 98-094. By Laura J. Horn. Project officer: C. Dennis Carroll. Washington, DC: Author.

National Center for Education Statistics. (2000). *Digest of Education Statistics 2000.* NCES 2001-034. Washington DC: Office of Education Research and Improvement, US Department of Education.

National Center for Education Statistics. (2001). *Students whose parents did not go to college: Postsecondary access, persistence and attainment.* NCES 2001-126. By S. Choy. Washington, DC: Author.

National Center for Education Statistics. (2002). *Digest of Education Statistics, 2001.* Washington, DC: Office of Education Research and Improvement, U.S. Department of Education.

Mortenson, T. (2001, October). Family income and higher education opportunity, 1970 to 2000. *Postsecondary Education OPPORTUNITY,* 112.

Mortenson, T. (2002, June). College continuation rates for recent high school graduates 1959 to 2001. *Postsecondary Education OPPORTUNITY*, 120.

Paulsen, M., & St. John, E. P. (1997). The financial nexus between college choice and persistence. In R. A. Vorhees (Ed.), Researching student aid: Creating an action agenda (Vol. 95. *New directions for institutional research*). San Francisco: Jossey Bass.

Paulsen, M., St. John, E. P., & Carter, D. F. (2002). *Diversity, college costs, and postsecondary opportunity: An examination of the financial nexus between college choice and persistence* (Policy Research Report #02-01). Bloomington, IN: Indiana Education Policy Center, Indiana University.

St. John, E. P. (2002). *The access challenge: Rethinking the causes of the new inequality* (Policy Issue Report # 2002-01). Bloomington, IN: Indiana University.

St. John, E. P. (2003). *Refinancing the college dream: Access, equal opportunity, and justice for taxpayers*. Baltimore: Johns Hopkins University Press.

St. John, E. P., Musoba, G. D., Simmons, A. B., Chung, C. G., Schmit, J., & Peng, C. J. (in press). Meeting the access challenge: An examination of Indiana's Twenty-first Century Scholars Program. Research in Higher Education. *Research in Higher Education.*

St. John, E. P., & Noell, J. (1989). The impact of financial aid on access: An analysis of progress with special consideration of minority access. *Research in Higher Education, 30*(6): 563-582.

St. John, E. P., Paulsen, M., & Starkey, J. B. (1996). The nexus between college choice and persistence. *Research in Higher Education, 37*(2), 175-220.

Terenzini, P. T., Cabrera, A. F., & Bernal, E. M. (2001). *Swimming against the tide: The poor in American higher education* (Research Report College Board Research Report No. 2001-1). New York: College Entrance Examination Board.

Tierney, W. G., & Hagedorn, L. S. (Eds.). (2002). *Increasing access to college: Extending possibilities for all students*. Albany, NY: State University of New York.

van der Klaauw, W. (2002). Estimating the effect of financial aid offers on college enrollment: A regression-discounting approach. *International Economic Review, November*, 1249-1288.

Venezia, A., Kirst, M. W., & Antonio, A. L. (2003, March 4, 2003). *Betraying the college dream: How disconnected K-12 and postsecondary education systems undermine student aspirations.* [Final policy report from Stanford University's Bridge Project]. The Bridge Project, Stanford University. Retrieved May 7, 2003, from http://bridgeproject.stanford.edu

SECTION III

Conclusion

CHAPTER 9

PUBLIC POLICY AND RESEARCH ON COLLEGE ACCESS: LESSONS LEARNED FROM FEDERAL ACCESS RESEARCH AND STATE EVALUATION STUDIES

Edward P. St. John

This volume of *Readings on Equal Education* has examined the role research plays in federal policy on access and presented evaluation studies of the effects of state policies and programs on access and equal education opportunity. Three decades ago the primary federal role in higher education was to provide student aid programs that helped equalize the opportunity to attend college while states provided opportunities by funding public systems of higher education. In recent decades, the federal government has deemphasized the equal opportunity goal of student aid in favor of encouraging academic preparation for college. The chapters in Section I clearly document that serious statistical errors were made in federally funded access and persistence reports that promoted this new agenda (Becker, Chapter 3; Heller, Chapter 2). These errors found their way into key non-government analyses of access and persistence that used these access and persistence reports to promote new political agendas for higher education. While the American Council for Education (ACE) once provided leadership in documenting the new inequality in higher education opportunity (e.g., Wilson, 1986), this national lobbying organization recently released a summary of ten years of federally funded access and persistence research that went so far as to argue that need-based aid was adequate (Choy, 2002).

In similar fashion, federally funded research on access was often used to inform policy development in states, as public officials tried to shape policies that expanded access to higher education. The evaluation studies in Section II reveal that serious problems emerged as a consequence of basing policy on reports with serious statistical errors. The federal access and persistence research was used in states to build rationales for merit grant programs (Heller, Chapter 5), to justify minimal investment in need-based grants as tuition charges rose in response to declining state subsidies (St. John & Chung, Chapter 6), and to promote school reforms that restricted opportunities to complete high school (St. John & Musoba, Chapter 7) strategies that have worsened the equity gap over the past few decades. There are glimmers of hope in state-level programs that encourage low-income students to prepare for college and provide adequate aid for low-income students (Musoba, Chapter 8), but too few states have initiated these reform strategies.

Given this troubling new context for public policy on college access, it is critical to rethink the role research plays in informing public policy, as well as to consider how research can inform policy development in states and at the federal level. As a conclusion, this chapter undertakes these tasks.

Finding Balance in Policy Research

This volume reveals the compelling need for balanced research on college access that considers plausible explanations for the disparity in the opportunity to enroll in college. There are three critical issues that researchers should consider in their efforts to improve research on college access.

Lesson 1: Researchers must recognize the limitations of extant databases and of statistical methods.

The chapters in Section I reviewed federal studies conducted by well qualified contractors. The reports reviewed introduced new concepts about the roles of high school courses into the policy discourse, but the methods had serious limitations. The reanalysis of the statistics on access (Fitzgerald, chapter 1), the reviews of the reports (Heller, chapter 2; Becker, chapter 3), and the preliminary reanalysis of NELS (Lee, chapter 4) were originally written at the request of the Advisory Committee on Student Financial Assistance, a Congressional Panel, and presented at national meetings of policymakers and researchers, in an effort to open up the national conversation about equal access. However, no attempt has ever been made to provide any sort of errata for these federal studies, which continue to be widely cited in policy documents. In particular, both Heller (Chapter 2) and Becker (Chapter 3) reveal serious problems with omitted variables bias and endogeneity.

In a recent research paper using the NELS database for research on access, DesJardins, McCall, Ahlburg, & Moore (2002) made the two critical observations. First, they pointed to the serious problems facing researchers using national databases:

> Many social scientists (including the authors of this article) are guilty of not remedying these endogeneity problems, and this is true with respect to models of student choice, performance, and departure. Many times variables such as whether a student delays entry, attends college full or part time, lives in an on-campus residence hall, or takes high levels of mathematics in high school are used to explain student success or failure in college. For instance, using the highest level of mathematics to explain whether a student graduates may contaminate the results since students who take advanced courses in mathematics probably intend to go to college and/or are more able and motivated than other students. (p. 107)

Second, they also argued that: "Given the importance of financial aid, NCES needs to find a better way to incorporate the longitudinal aid data" (p. 109). The failure to provide adequate data on financial aid does not absolve the agency of responsibility for assessing the effects of student aid on access, or for controlling for the effects of family income when considering the factors that influence of academic preparation. Instead, other means for controlling for the role of student aid should be considered, such as incorporating measures related to state funding for grants (Chapter 6) into multilevel access and persistence models that use the longitudinal databases.

Thus the essays in this volume are not alone in pointing to the serious problems facing researchers who work with national databases to examine the factors that predict college enrollment, persistence, and performance. Since federal and state policymakers propose new policies—such as new educational standards or merit scholarships—based on rationalizations that these solutions will improve educational outcomes, it is incumbent on the research community to conduct evaluative research in spite of these potential data limitations. However, appropriate caution should be used when making claims about what is explained and unexplained by their statistical analyses.

Lesson 2: Theory and prior research should inform the development of statistical models for research on college access when they use statistical analyses to explain the predictors of college enrollment and persistence.

The reviews of NCES studies by Fitzgerald (Chapter 1), Heller (Chapter 2), and Becker (Chapter 3) reveal the severe limitation of federally funded research on access in the U.S. And while the state-level studies in Section II provide insight into how more balance could be achieved, this issue merits further elaboration, building on the important points made by the contributing authors. All of the contributors worked with widely accepted theories on attainment and access, many of the prior studies using the federal databases ignored sound theory and drew faulty statistical inferences with gravely incorrect policy conclusions. A set of subsidiary lessons should inform the development of statistical models used to assess the impact of public policies on college access.

Lesson 2.1:   Social theory and research should inform the selection and interpretation of variables related to family background and encouragement.

First, the long-standing research on social attainment and economics of education demonstrate a strong relationship between parents' education and family income. It is extremely difficult to untangle the distinct effects of the two types of variables. The statistical errors made by these federal contractors are rooted in the failure to recognize the roles of income and parents' education as related aspects of social class (Becker, Chapter 3; Heller, Chapter 2). In addition, Musoba (Chapter 8) demonstrated that encouragement also plays a crucial role in the formation of aspirations, as evidenced by decisions to apply for student aid. This proposition is now well established in theory and research on social capital and therefore merits consideration in future efforts to analyze the effects of policy on college access.

Lesson 2.2: Economic theory and research should inform research on the effects of financial aid.

It is startling that researchers studying college access for a federal agency could overlook thirty years of economic research on student demand, but there is overwhelming evidence of this fundamental mistake in access and persistence studies (see chapters in Section I). As William Becker (Chapter 3) points out, the analysis of the role of financial aid in access is complicated because aid eligibility is not evident unless students have applied for aid. However, although analyses of enrollment by applicants can inform policy and have been used for several decades in evaluation research using NCES databases (e.g., Jackson, 1978, 1988; St. John, 1990, 1991), the NCES and its contractors failed to take this step. Instead, they argued that there was equal opportunity without considering the direct effects of student aid (Heller, Chapter 2), a fatally flawed approach to policy research. While further refinement in the methods used to predict aid eligibility is possible (Becker, Chapter 3) and is especially needed in cases of merit aid programs and hybrid programs that combine merit and need, it is possible to assess the direct effects of aid when researchers pay attention to the aid application process (e.g., Musoba, Chapter 8).

In addition, some of the authors used alternative approaches for assessing the impact of student aid. Heller (Chapter 5) reviewed studies developed from the Harvard Civil Rights Project that systematically examined the impact of merit grants by comparing states. The Indiana research team used a state-level model to assess the impact of need-based and non-need (merit) grants on high school graduation and enrollment rates in states. These studies demonstrate it is possible to assess the direct effects of student aid.

Lesson 2.3: Education theory and research can inform the development of statistical models that assess the role of high school curriculum in promoting college access.

While Clifford Adelman (1995, 1999) has made a substantial contribution to the research community by developing student records on high school courses in NCES databases, using an academic index to screen out most low-income students in analyses of the effects of family income is fatally flawed (Becker, Chapter 3). John Lee (Chapter 4) demonstrated that by using course-related variables it is possible to control for preparation in a straightforward way. Given the many statistical errors in the NCES efforts to manipulate student-level data on high school courses and applications (Becker, Chapter 3; Heller, Chapter 2), it is crucial that policy researchers begin the difficult process of theorizing the role of high school courses in the academic preparation process, considering the impact of family background and aid on preparation. The NCES studies essentially treated a qualification index as a mega-level variable that combined student behavior and policy related variables.   As Becker illustrated (Chapter 3), by using such a convoluted variable, NCES obfuscated the effects of academic policies and family background on the preparation process, clearly pointing to the need for better delineation between course-level variables and policy variables.

The analysis of academic access (St. John et al., Chapter 7) illustrated an approach that can be used to assess the effect of state-level policy variables on test scores, high school graduation, and college enrollment. Clearly public policy influences both achievement and opportunity (St. John, 2003) and it is critical that researchers examine both types of effects. By narrowly defining the outcomes of policies related to preparation—and by creating an index that excludes people who lacked the opportunity to prepare for college—this body of research misled states. It is crucial that states begin to assess the effect of their educational policies on both equity and achievement outcomes. The national goals should be to improve both equity and achievement, rather than to push children out of the educational system who do not measure up to artificial correlates of academic success.

Lesson 2.4: Financial aid must be included in federal policy research that considers college access.

There is substantial evidence that family finances—and concern about net costs of college—influence whether students complete high school and prepare for college (St. John & Chung, Chapter 6). It is misleading to assume that schools' contexts—or parents' education—alone can explain variations in preparation, given the substantial direct effect of college costs and student aid on preparation during and graduation from high school. In addition, federal policy researchers who are examining the association between academic preparation and access—i.e., the influence of courses students taken in high school—must also consider the role of financial aid. This is necessary because the reports on preparation have so frequently used their analyses to claim that preparation explains disparity in access. However, if the role of financial aid (or of net cost) is not considered, it is impossible to make valid inferences about the effects of family income and other variables related to family income, such as parents' education and academic preparation.

Lesson 3: Policy researchers should use balanced approaches to the development of statistical models and the interpretation of the statistics.

While NCES made serious statistical errors in its studies of access and persistence, this failure is not as problematic as the bias that underlies these faulty choices about variables and the interpretation of results. There was a paradigm shift in the last two decades, from policies motivated by equity considerations to policies driven by excellence considerations. It is critical that researchers evolve analytic models and theoretical perspectives that recognize the intent of both finance and education policies, since both types of policies influence college access.

Brian Fitzgerald (Chapter 1) and the Advisory Committee on Student Financial Assistance (2001, 2002) have provided national leadership in efforts to find a new, more balanced approach to policy research on college access, the more critical policy issue. The major breakthrough in the Advisory Committee's approach was to use statistics on academic preparation from tables in these federal access reports to illustrate that the text of these reports overlooked that a large number of college-prepared students who failed to enroll in college. John Lee (Chapter 4) further illustrates the magnitude of this oversight in his preliminary reanalysis of NELS. He further documents that a large number of low-income students lacked the opportunity to attend college. Thus, whether or not the reported statistics are used (Fitzgerald, Chapter 1), or the databases are reanalyzed (Lee, Chapter 4), the results contradict the conclusions the researchers reached when interpreting their own statistics. Because of these statistical errors (Becker, Chapter 3; Heller, Chapter 2) and misinterpretations of their own reported statistics (Fitzgerald, Chapter 1; Lee, Chapter 4), these reports demonstrated a clear bias, an unsubstantiated belief that academic preparation explained the entirety of inequality in access, leaving nothing for finances to explain.

As Becker's paper so clearly illustrated (Chapter 3), it was a mistake for the federal researchers to overlook the influence of family finances on the opportunity to prepare for college or enroll in college. But even though they used this unfair standard, these researchers failed to recognize a clear pattern in the statistics they reported: a large number of low-income students were left behind (Fitzgerald, Chapter 1). Researchers need a balanced frame of reference to develop sound statistical models and to present fair interpretations of statistical results, minimal standards that federal access and persistence studies clearly failed to meet.

New Directions in Public Policy

The flawed research on college access and persistence is a reflection of a dominant political belief that schools are failing children and school failure explains the access challenge. This point of view not only dominated public policy at the state and federal level during the last few decades (Miron & St. John, 2003), but it dominated federal research leading to statistical errors and misinterpretation of statistical results. Clearly official policy research literature, represented by the NCES studies of access and related reports by ACE (Choy, 2002; Gladieux & Swail, 1999; King, 1999), has promoted a reform agenda that emphasized encouraging—and even requiring—students to take advanced courses in high school, as the primary means of expanding college access. This strategy may have contributed to the improvement in the rate of college enrollment by high school graduates in the U.S. (St. John, 2003), but the research reported in this volume does not fully support this hypothesis (Chapter 7). Given the failure of so many researchers to consider the consequences of reductions in federal grant aid, along with the ambiguous results of the academic policies NCES research supports, it is important to reflect on the policy lessons learned from the research using a balanced approach, including the chapters in this volume.

Lesson 4: Measures of equal access must be more carefully defined and should be used if there are efforts to expand public accountability systems in higher education.

The federal reports reviewed in Section I advanced a very narrow notion of access that was misleading and that continues to mislead educational policy formulation. Specifically, the federal reports attempted to explain away differences in college enrollment by sorting students based on their qualifications, but their qualifications were influenced by the finance variables they omitted or failed to consider fully. This approach ignores three critical issues substantiated by research in the volume, supplemented by thirty plus years of empirical evidence on college access:

1. Student aid and family income have an indirect effect on preparation and high school graduation by low-income students.
2. Student aid has a direct effect on the opportunity of low-income students to apply for, enroll in, and persist in college, especially for low-income students.
3. In the 1970s, there was greater equality in college enrollment rates across diverse ethnic groups and between income groups than there has been for the past two decades.

Given these understandings it is important that policy studies of college assess equity in access across different income and ethnic groups, as well as the rate of college enrollment. Nor can access be reduced to the rates of enrollment for groups that meet a predetermined set of academic criteria, because it is virtually impossible to identify measures of preparation that are not determined, at least in part, by family resources, access to quality education, and the ability to pay for college. Clearly the steps necessary to prepare for college, from taking the right courses to applying for college, are influenced by family income and financial aid. Equal access cannot be achieved unless the financial barriers to academic preparation are removed, along with the financial barriers to enrollment. At the current time, there is evidence that there are barriers to preparation (Chapter 7) and to financial access (Chapter 6).

As the federal government moves toward a national system of accountability that includes measures of access and persistence, a possible outcome of the next reauthorization of the *Higher Education Act*, it is crucial that these measures be adjusted for the impact of federal aid—and the potential inadequacy of this aid—as well as for the impact of college prices and state grant aid (St. John, Kline, and Asker, 2001). The current efforts to develop and use accountability measures in higher education overlook the concept of equal access, a measured comparison of enrollment and/or persistence rates for diverse groups. Further, it is impossible to hold institutions responsible for the failure of low-income students to attain educationally when their inability to enroll or persist is the product of inadequate government funding for need-based grants. Clearly there is a need to rethink the role of accountability schemes based on a better definition of equal access, one that considers the inherent inequality in the public system of higher education finance. Given the state of unequal access, a situation more at least partially attributable to government policy, it is reckless to tie funding to persistence measures unless adequate student aid is provided. It is necessary to use routine reporting on unequal and to hold states and the federal government accountable for their failure to make a sufficient investment before it is possible to construct accountability measures that are workable to use as a basis for institutional funding.

Lesson 5: States should evaluate the effects of education reforms that emphasize academic preparation on inequality in post-secondary opportunity as well as on student achievement.
While there is mixed evidence about the effects of higher standards and more restrictive requirements on student achievement, it is clear that these policies are associated with the lower high school graduation rates (St. John et. al, Chapter 7). The analysis of academic access revealed an association between several recent reforms and SAT scores, but these reforms were associated with lower high school graduation rates and did not have a significant association with college enrollment. These results indicate that policymakers should systematically evaluate the effects of their state policies on high school graduation, considering both equity and achievement outcomes, before continuing down the path of using high standards to regulate schools and testing to hold them accountable. While improving achievement of high school students is desirable, it is not clear that the current approaches are working. Not only have the flawed national access studies have been used to promote academic preparation as the solution to the access challenge, but also these new rationales are flawed because they are based on faulty foundations.
Policymakers in many states have used these misleading statistical analyses—for example, the correlation between high school algebra and college enrollment—to rationalize policies that require advanced math for high school graduation. Policymakers who hold this belief should ponder the statistical errors revealed by Heller (Chapter 2) and Becker (Chapter 3). The methods used in these studies were flawed. Lee's preliminary reanalysis revealed

that many qualified students have been left behind due to finances (Chapter 4). Thus, even if these policies do have a positive influence on achievement—and there is sound evidence to support this proposition (St. John et al., Chapter 7)—there are still large numbers of qualified students left behind. If these policies actually improved the number of students who prepared, then logically we would expect more students to be left behind, increasing the negative effect of false promises embedded in this policy approach. This is not to argue that school reforms don't work, but the research clearly illustrates that educational reforms in high schools do not solve the financial access problem.

The effects of education reforms are seldom studied, but should be systematically and routinely evaluated. Evaluators and researchers should use balanced approaches in evaluation studies that examine the effects of state policies, a step that could make it easier for voters to hold public officials accountable when their policies fail. There is a strong espoused belief in accountability built into educational policy, but a blatant failure to evaluate the effects of those policies. The methodology used in evaluating the impact of state education policies (St. John et al., Chapter 7) can be used to develop state profiles that document the role of policies in each state. Such an approach to state reports merits consideration.

Lesson 6: Since adequate need-based financial aid is necessary to ensure financial access, states and the federal government should collaborate on new financial strategies to achieve this goal.

Education reforms would be more successful in promoting equal access if there was adequate need-based student grant aid available to low- and moderate-income students who prepare for college (Fitzgerald, Chapter 2; St. John et al., Chapter 6). Based on reexaminations of access and persistence studies (Fitzgerald, Chapter 1; Lee, Chapter 4), the Advisory Committee on Student Financial Assistance (2002) has estimated that four million students will be left behind in the early 21st century because of inadequate student aid. The studies on state aid policy in this volume (Heller, Chapter 2; St. John et al., Chapter 6) indicate that need-based grants are the best means to ensure financial access for low-income students.

Given the rise in public college tuition charges (St. John et al., Chapter 6), it is critical that states and the federal government share responsibility for ensuring financial access. In the 1960s and 1970s, when the federal need-based programs were being developed and implemented, college tuition charges did not increase substantially (St. John, 1994). However, given the substantial rise in public colleges since 1980, it is critical that states and the federal government collaborate on fixing the problem, possibly sharing the costs of a second tier of grant aid (St. John, 2003; St. John & Chung, Wooden, & Mendez, in press). Regardless of the specific strategy used to improve need-based aid, this issue should have high priority on the policy agenda at the federal level and in most states.

Lesson 7: Encouragement programs can increase preparation and, if there is adequate need-based grant aid, improve college enrollment.

There is evidence that a comprehensive approach that combines encouragement to prepare with adequate student financial aid represents a viable approach to expanding college access. Musoba (Chapter 8) demonstrates that Indiana's Twenty-first Century Scholars Program has a substantial impact on expanding enrollment opportunities for African Americans and Whites, but even this exemplary program can be improved upon. The program incorporates outreach to parents as well as to high school students, encouraging parents to become engaged in the college choice process. In combination, this study indicates that encouragement is appropriate when linked to student aid.

Conclusion

Access research is at a crossroads, reflecting the ambiguous state of public policy on college access. For the past two decades, the federal government overlooked the role of financial aid as their reports used dubious statistical methods and flawed theories of access to tell an incomplete story about how the new access challenge could be solved. It is time to rethink the role of policy research, just as it is crucial for states and the federal government to collaborate on new approaches to ensuring equal access for students who prepare for college.

This examination of access and persistence studies revealed that a large number of low- and moderate-income college-qualified students were behind due to inadequate student aid (Fitzgerald, Chapter 1; Lee, Chapter 4). This was evident in tables from in these federal access and persistence reports even though this conclusion seldom was mentioned in those reports. Further, the reports contained statistical errors, along with the serious misinterpretations of the reported statistics. These reports told the story that the inequality in access was attributed to low level of parent education and poor quality of preparation, but this conclusion turned out to be fictional. Not only were many of the statistics in the reports wrong (Becker, Chapter 3; Heller, Chapter 2), but the conclusions in these reports did not accurately reflect the findings on family income and student aid that were evident in their own tables (Fitzgerald, Chapter 1; Heller, Chapter 2). State policies that have been based on the federal access studies should be evaluated and improved upon.

The evaluation studies reported in this volume reveal that the new reforms implemented based on the academic preparation rationale have had mixed effects. The merit aid programs improved enrollment in public colleges, but added to the inequality in access (Heller, Chapter 5). The failure to invest in need-based grant aid further increased the disparity, adding to the inequality (Chapter 6). The new educational reforms were associated with higher test scores, but did not influence college enrollment rates for high school graduates. These reforms apparently reduced high school graduation rates (Chapter 7). Thus, not only were the new reform policies built on a fiction (and flawed research), but they did not have their intended effects.

If the new reforms—the higher standards, testing, and merit aid programs—are carried forward, they should be routinely evaluated. The evaluation results should be used to reform the reforms—that is, to promote continuous improvement. The idea that government programs should be routinely evaluated was built into the systematic education reforms in the 1960s and 1970s (Schultz, 1968; Weathersby & Balderston, 1972). Even if these systems approaches gave way to new politically motivated reforms based on new ideologies, evaluation remains critical. Unfortunately, in recent times federal research has been used to tell fictional stories, creating the false record on educational progress, rather than to provide reliable evaluations.

The message from this volume is simple: both policymakers and policy researchers need to seek reliable information about the effects of public policies, rather than continue to misuse statistics to support false claims based supported by flawed statistics. The shift from beliefs driving research to realistic evaluations is critical in the domain of college access. The education reforms of the 1990s were based on a false message: the espoused beliefs about academic preparation overshadowed the realities on financial inequality in college opportunity. The challenge of finding a balanced approach to education reform and public finance must be met or the dream that education as an avenue for upward mobility will be lost for another generation of Americans.

References

Adelman, C. (1995). *The new college course map and transcript files: Changes in course-taking and achievement, 1972-1993.* Washington, DC: National Center for Education Statistics.

Adelman, C. (1999). *Answers in the tool box: Academic intensity, attendance patterns, and bachelor's degree attainment.* Washington, DC: National Center for Education Statistics.

Advisory Committee on Student Financial Assistance. (2001). *Access denied: Restoring equal educational opportunity.* Washington, DC: Author.

Advisory Committee on Student Financial Assistance. (2002). *Empty promises: The myth of college access in America.* Washington, DC: Author.

Choy, S. P. (2002). *Access & persistence: Findings from 10 years of longitudinal research on students.* Washington, DC: American Council on Education.

DesJardins, S. L., McCall, B. P., Ahlburg, D. A., & Moye, M. J. (2002). Adding a timing light to the 'tool box.' *Journal of Higher Education, 43,* 83-114.

Gladieux, L. E., & Swail, W. S. (1999). Financial aid is not enough: Improving the odds for low-income and minority students. In *Financing a college education: How it works, how it is changing,* In J. E. King (Ed.), (pp. 177-197). Phoenix, AZ: Oryx Press.

Jackson, G. A. (1978). Financial aid and student enrollment. *Journal of Higher Education, 49,* 548-574.

Jackson, G. A. (1988). Did college choice change during the seventies? *Economics of Education Review, 7,* 15-27.

King, J. E. (Ed.) 1999. *Financing a college education: How it works, how it is changing.* Phoenix, AZ: Oryx Press.

Miron, L. F., & St. John, E. P. (Eds.). (2003). *Reinterpreting urban school reforms: Have urban schools failed, or has the reform movement failed urban schools?* Albany: State University of New York Press.

Schultz, C. (1968). *The politics of public spending.* Washington, DC: The Brookings Institution.

St. John, E. P. (1990). Price response in enrollment decisions: An analysis of the High School and Beyond sophomore cohort. *Research in Higher Education, 31*(2), 161-176.

St. John, E. P. (1991). What really influences minority student attendance? An analysis of the High School and Beyond sophomore cohort. *Research in Higher Education, 32*(2), 141-158.

St. John, E. P. (1994). *Prices, productivity and investment: Assessing financial strategies in higher education.* ASHE/ERIC Higher Education Report, No. 3. Washington, DC: George Washington University.

St. John, E. P. (2003). *Refinancing the college dream: Access, equal opportunity, and justice for taxpayers.* Baltimore: Johns Hopkins University Press.

St. John, E. P., Chung, C. G., Musoba, G. D., Simmons, A. B., Wooden, O. S., & Mendez, J. (In press). *Expanding college access: The impact of state finance strategies.* Indianapolis: The Lumina Foundation for Education.

St. John, E. P., Kline, K. & Asker, E. H. (2001). The call for public accountability: Rethinking the linkage to student outcomes. In *The states and public higher education policy: Access, Affordability, and Accountability,* ed. D. H. Heller, 219-242, Baltimore: Johns Hopkins University Press.

Weathersby, G. B., and F. E. Balderston. (1972). PPBS in higher education planning and management: Part I, an overview. *Higher Education, 1,* 191-206.

Wilson, R. (1986). *Overview of the issue: Minority/poverty student enrollment problems.* Paper presented at the NASSG/NCHELP Conference on Student Financial Aid Research, Third Annual in Chicago, IL.